FORESTRY COMMISSION BULLETIN 123

Managing Rides, Roadsides and Edge Habitats in Lowland Forests

Richard Ferris[1] and Clive Carter[2]

[1]*Woodland Ecology Branch*, [2]*formerly Entomology Branch, Forest Research, Alice Holt Lodge, Wrecclesham, Farnham, Surrey GU10 4LH*

D1437444

Edinburgh: Forestry Commission

ISBN 0 85538 415 8

Ferris, R.; Carter, C. 2000
Managing Rides, Roadsides and Edge Habitats in Lowland Forests. Bulletin 123.
Forestry Commission, Edinburgh. xxii + 86

FDC   267:907.1:18:15:(410)

KEYWORDS: Conservation, Forestry, Rides, Roadsides, Edges, Open areas, Succession, Vegetation management

Acknowledgements

The authors would like to thank the many people in Forest Enterprise who have shared their experience of managing edges and open areas, particularly staff of Northants, South-East England, and The New Forest Districts. Thanks are also due to Fred Currie, Wildlife and Conservation Officer, Forestry Commission (England), for comments on an earlier draft of the Bulletin; Jenny Claridge for editing and overseeing the project through to completion; John Williams and George Gate for producing the artwork; and The Royal Greenwich Observatory for developing ideas about light modelling. The original project was conceived by Mark Anderson, and his role and that of Peter Buckley (Wye College, University of London) in making this Bulletin possible is gratefully acknowledged.

Front cover: Sunlit forest edge with high floristic diversity, Bentley Wood, Wiltshire. (C.I.CARTER) *inset* Silver-washed fritillary, *Argynnis paphia.* (C.I.CARTER)

Back cover: A sunny rideside bay in a Corsican pine plantation, Pembrey Forest, Dyfed. (R.FERRIS) *left inset* Ride mowing in a lowland beechwood, Micheldever, Hampshire. (R.FERRIS) *right inset* Primrose *(Primula vulgaris)*, a woodland plant and important food source for the Duke of Burgundy fritillary *(Hamearis lucina)* which may benefit from ride or roadside management. (R.FERRIS)

Enquiries relating to this publication should be addressed to:
The Research Communications Officer
Forest Research
Alice Holt Lodge
Wrecclesham, Farnham
Surrey GU10 4LH

Contents

List of plates

List of figures

Managing Rides, Roadsides and Edge Habitats in Lowland Forests

Summary

Rides, roadsides and edges are important habitats in forests. Their priority in forest management for conservation is further emphasised by *The UK forestry standard* statement on the importance of '...maintenance, conservation and appropriate enhancement of biological diversity in forest ecosystems...' as a key criterion in sustainable forest management. Forest edge species are particularly important in British forests. This is largely because historical forest fragmentation and silvicultural regimes based on coppicing and wood pasture favoured edge species and maintained unnaturally high populations which, today, are of conservation importance. The same historical trends resulted in a decline in forest interior habitats and species which should not be overlooked in management planning. Edge habitats in plantations often form interlinked networks of roads, rides, watercourses, wayleaves, operational open space and stand boundaries which enhance their conservation value. They can serve as refugia for recolonisation of felled or thinned stands.

Forest edges have particular microclimatic conditions which are favourable to many species of conservation importance. These arise mainly from the availability of direct sunlight and shelter. They are generally subject to successional processes, leading to colonisation and establishment of woodland, although these are likely to be modified or arrested by herbivores. Manipulation of light, microclimate and vegetation succession are the basis for management of edges for several purposes: to create diverse and species rich edge habitats, to provide for the needs of particular species groups, or to maintain semi-natural open habitats.

A clear management strategy with specific targets is essential to focus management efforts. This will be influenced by judgements of what is feasible, ecologically appropriate, cost-effective, affordable and compatible with other management objectives, over the time scale required for the desired benefits to accrue. The process must begin with an objective assessment of management potential, both ecological, organisational and financial. Once the potential is established, a design and management approach can be formulated. This Bulletin provides information on the ecological value and management of rides, roadsides and edge habitats. Part One describes the ecology of edges and open areas. It looks at their value in both semi-natural and plantation woodland, and discusses the influences of light and microclimate, vegetation succession and wildlife. Part Two provides a guide to edge management options, including practical advice on strategy, design, maintenance of vegetation zones and monitoring.

La gestion des habitats formés par les allées cavalières, bords de route et lisières des forêts de plaine

Résumé

Les allées cavalières, bords de routes et lisières constituent des habitats importants au sein des forêts. L'importance prioritaire qui leur est accordée dans la gestion forestière soucieuse de conservation se trouve encore soulignée par l' *UK forestry standard* qui énonce l'importance 'du maintien, de la conservation et de l'accroissement approprié de la diversité biologique des écosystèmes forestiers...' en tant que critère clé d'une gestion forestière durable. Les essences poussant à la lisière des forêts sont particulièrement importantes dans les forêts britanniques. Ceci s'explique en grande partie par le fait que le morcellement de la forêt et le recours à des régimes de sylviculture reposant sur l'élagage et les pâturages boisés ont historiquement favorisé les essences poussant en lisière et maintenu des populations anormalement élevées qu'il est de nos jours important de protéger. Ces mêmes tendances historiques ont amené le déclin des habitats et essences trouvés à l'intérieur des forêts, ce qui ne devrait pas être négligé dans l'élaboration des plans de gestion. Dans les plantations, les habitats de lisière forment souvent des réseaux entrecroisés de routes, allées cavalières, cours d'eau, droits de passages, espaces verts de manoeuvre et limites de peuplement, ce qui accroît leur valeur du point de vue de la conservation. Ils peuvent servir de refuges pour les organismes vivants, permettant la recolonisation des peuplements abattus ou éclaircis.

Les lisières de forêt bénéficient de conditions microclimatiques particulières qui sont favorables à de nombreuses essences importantes à conserver. Ceci est surtout dû au fait qu'elles jouissent de lumière solaire directe et d'une situation abritée. Elles sont généralement sujettes à des processus de succession amenant à la colonisation et à l'établissement de bois, bien que ces processus puissent être modifiés ou arrêtés par les herbivores. La manipulation de la lumière, le microclimat et la succession végétale sont les bases sur lesquelles se fonde une gestion des lisières répondant à plusieurs objectifs: créer des habitats de lisière diverses et riches en essences, subvenir aux besoins de groupes d'essences particulières ou maintenir des habitats découverts semi-naturels.

Une stratégie de gestion clairement définie se donnant des objectifs spécifiques est essentielle pour focaliser les efforts de gestion. Cette stratégie sera influencée par ce que l'on aura jugé faisable, approprié sur le plan écologique, rentable, abordable et compatible avec les autres objectifs de la gestion, dans le temps requis pour que les bénéfices désirés s'accumulent. Ce processus doit commencer par une évaluation objective du potentiel de gestion, à la fois écologique, organisationnel et financier. Une fois ce potentiel établi, il sera possible de formuler un plan et une démarche de gestion. Ce bulletin fournit des renseignements sur la valeur et la gestion écologiques des habitats constitués par les allées cavalières, bordures de routes et lisières. La Première Partie décrit l'écologie des lisières et des espaces découverts. Elle examine leur valeur au sein des bois semi-naturels et des plantations forestières, et discute les influences de la lumière et du microclimat, la succession végétale, la faune et la flore sauvages. La Deuxième Partie fournit un guide présentant des options de gestion adaptées aux lisières et comportant des conseils pratiques englobant stratégie, conception, entretien des zones de végétation et suivi.

Bewirtschaftung von Scheisen, Straßenrändern und Randbiotopen in Tieflandwäldern

Zusammenfassung

Schneisen, Straßenränder und Grenzen bilden im Wald wichtige Lebensräume. Der 'U.K. Fortswirtschaftsstandardbericht' unterstreicht ihre Priorität innerhalb der Forstbewirtschaftung, indem er 'Erhalt, Schutz und angepasste Förderung von biologischer Vielfalt in Waldökosystemen' als Schlüsselfaktor für nachhaltigen Forstbetrieb beschreibt. Waldrandarten sind in britischen Wäldern besonders wichtig. Die Gründe dafür liegen in der historisch bedingten Waldfragmentierung und forstlichen Methoden die auf Kopfholz- und Waldweidenwirtschaft zurückgehen. Dies förderte Waldrandarten und damit unnatürlich hohe Populationen, die heutzutage sehr große Bedeutung für den Umweltschutz haben. Die gleichen historischen Trends führten zur Verkümmerung der Lebensräume und Artenvielfalt im Waldesinneren, und dies sollte inbezug des Bewirtschaftungsplanes nicht unbeachtet bleiben. Randlebensräume in Anpflanzungen bilden oft ein Verbundnetz von Straßen, Schneisen, Wasserläufen, Wegerechten, offenen Arbeitsräumen und Standgrenzen und dies erhöht ihren Naturschutzwert. Sie können außerdem als Schutzraum zur Wiederbesiedlung von gefällten oder ausgedünnten Ständen wirken.

Waldränder besitzen bestimmte, mikroklimatische Bedingungen, die viele Arten, deren Erhaltung wichtig ist, fördern. Diese Bedingungen sind meist aufgrund des Vorhandenseins von direktem Sonnenlicht und Deckung. Diese Ränder unterliegen Nachfolgeprozessen, die zur Kolonisierung und Waldetablierung führen, obwohl dies wahrscheinlich durch Äsung modifiziert oder gestoppt würde. Die Manipulierung von Licht, Mikroklima und Pflanznachfolge bilden die Grundsteine zur Ränder-bewirtschaftung und erfüllen verschiedene Zwecke: Bildung von unterschiedlichen und artenreichen Randlebensräumen, Erschaffung von Bedingungen für bestimmte Artengruppen oder die Erhaltung halbnatürlicher, offener Lebensräume.

Ein klarer Bewirtschaftungsplan mit bestimmten Zielen ist absolut notwendig, um die Bewirtschaftungsanstrengungen zu konzentrieren. Dazu muß beurteilt werden, was machbar, ökologisch angebracht und kostengünstig ist. Der benötigte Zeitraum, um die erwünschten Nutzen zu erreichen, muß mit anderen Bewirtschaftungszielen kompatibel sein. Der Vorgang muß mit der objektiven Beurteilung des Bewirtschaftungspotentials, in ökologischer, organisatorischer und finanzieller Hinsicht, beginnen. Wenn dieses Potential besteht, kann ein Gestaltungs- und Bewirtschaftungsplan formuliert werden. Dieses Bulletin gibt Informationen über den ökologischen Wert und die Bewirtschaftung von Schneisen, Straßenrändern und Randbiotopen. Teil 1 beschreibt die Ökologie von Rändern und offenen Flächen. Es betrachtete ihren Wert innerhalb von halbwilden und Schonungswäldern, und diskutiert die Einflüße von Licht und Mikroklima, Pflanznachfolge und Wildfauna. Teil 2 gibt einen Auswahl von Randbewirtschaftungsmöglichkeiten, zusammen mit praktischen Ratschlägen hinsichtlich Strategie, Entwurf, Pflege der Pflanzzonen und Überwachung.

Rheoli Rhodfeydd, Ochrau ffyrdd a Chynefinoedd y Godreon mewn Coedwigoedd Tir Isel

Crynodeb

Mae rhodfeydd, ochrau ffyrdd a godreon yn gynefinoedd pwysig mewn coedwigoedd. Pwysleisir eu blaenoriaeth mewn rheolaeth coedwigoedd ar gyfer cadwraeth ymhellach gan ddatganiad *Safon coedwigaeth* y DU ar bwysigrwydd '...cynnal, gwarchod a chynyddu'n briodol yr amrywiaeth fiolegol mewn ecosystemau coedwig...' fel maen prawf allweddol mewn rheolaeth coedwigoedd gynaliadwy. Mae rhywogaethau godre'r goedwig o bwysigrwydd arbennig mewn coedwigoedd Prydeinig. Mae hyn yn bennaf oherwydd roedd darnio hanesyddol y coedwigoedd a threfnau tyfu coed wedi eu seilio ar goedlannau a phorfeydd coed oedd yn ffafrio rhywogaethau godre'r goedwig ac yn cynnal poblogaethau annaturiol o uchel sydd, heddiw, o bwysigrwydd cadwraethol. Un canlyniad o'r un tueddiadau hanesyddol oedd gostyngiad mewn cynefinoedd a rhywogaethau y tu mewn i'r goedwig na ddylid eu hanwybyddu wrth gynllunio rheolaeth. Yn aml mae cynefinoedd y godre mewn planhigfeydd yn ffurfio rhwydweithiau cysylltiedig o lonydd, rhodfeydd, cyrsiau dŵr, hawliau tramwy a therfynau mannau agored a chlystyrau coed gweithredol sy'n codi eu gwerth cadwraethol. Gallant fod o fudd fel llochesau ar gyfer ailgytrefu clystyrau o goed a dorrwyd i lawr neu a deneuwyd.

Mae amgylchiadau microhinsoddol neilltuol godreon y goedwig yn ffafriol i lawer rhywogaeth o bwysigrwydd cadwraethol. Deillia'r rhain yn bennaf o'r golau haul a'r lloches sydd ar gael. Yn gyffredinol mae godreon coedwigoedd yn rhwym wrth brosesau olyniaethol, sy'n arwain at gytrefu a sefydlu coetir, er gellir newid neu rwystro'r rhain gan lysysyddion. Mae dylanwadu ar olau, y microhinsawdd ac olyniaeth planhigion yn sail ar gyfer rheoli godreon at sawl diben: i greu cynefinoedd y godreon sy'n amrywiol ac amlrywogaethol, i ddiwallu anghenion grwpiau arbennig o rywogaethau, neu i gynnal cynefinoedd agored lled-naturiol.

Mae strategaeth reoli glir gyda thargedau penodol yn hanfodol er mwyn canolbwyntio ar ymdrechion rheolaeth. Dylanwadir ar hyn gan y farn o'r hyn sy'n bosibl, yn ecolegol briodol, yn gost-effeithiol, yn fforddiadwy ac yn gyson ag amcanion rheolaeth eraill, dros y raddfa amser sydd ei hangen er mwyn i'r buddion a ddymunir grynhoi. Mae'n rhaid i'r broses ddechrau gydag asesiad gwrthrychol o bosibiliadau rheolaeth, yn ecolegol, yn drefniadol ac yn ariannol. Unwaith y cadarnheir y posibiliadau, gellir ffurfio cynllun a dull rheoli. Mae'r Bwletin hwn yn rhoi gwybodaeth ar werth ecolegol a'r rheolaeth o rodfeydd, ochrau ffyrdd a chynefinoedd y godre. Mae Rhan 1 yn disgrifio ecoleg godreon a mannau agored. Mae'n edrych ar eu gwerth mewn coetir planhigfeydd a choetir lled-naturiol; hefyd mae'n trafod dylanwadau golau a'r microhinsawdd, olyniaeth planhigion a bywyd gwyllt. Mae Rhan Dau yn rhoi cyfarwyddyd ar ddewisiadau o ran rheoli godreon, gan gynnwys cyngor ymarferol ar strategaeth, cynllun, cynnal ardaloedd o lysdyfiant ac arolygu.

Chapter 1

Introduction

The need to conserve biological diversity *(biodiversity)* has been recognised for a considerable time, and has been implicitly reinforced through a wide range of national and international policy statements and legislation, for example the 1981 Wildlife and Countryside Act and its 1985 Amendment. However, the issues only really gained widespread recognition in their own right following The United Nations Conference on Environment and Development (UNCED), held in Rio de Janeiro in 1992 (Figure 1.1). This established the Convention on Biological Diversity. This convention sets out actions for each country involved, aimed at conserving biodiversity to ensure the sustainable use of species and habitats exploited by humankind. Each of the signatories agreed to develop national strategies, plans or programmes for the

conservation and sustainable use of biodiversity, for example *Biodiversity: the UK action plan* (UK Government, 1994a).

Within Europe, the Ministerial Conference on the Protection of Forests in Europe, held in Helsinki in June 1993, saw the development of The Resolution for the Conservation of Biodiversity of European Forests (Helsinki Guidelines). This resolution effectively bridges the gap between native, natural and managed forests and provides for the enhancement of biodiversity as part of sustainable management. In response to this, the UK Government published *Sustainable forestry: the UK programme* (UK Government, 1994b), which pulled together the various strands of forestry policy and programmes into a coherent whole, taking into account international principles

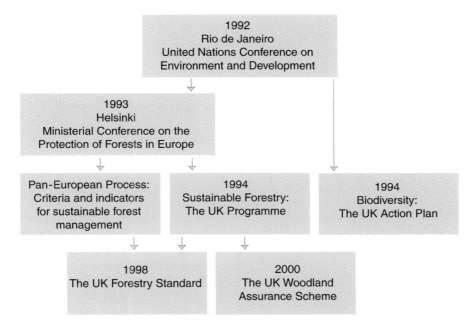

Figure 1.1 Important milestones in the development of sustainable forest management and biodiversity conservation as key objectives in UK forestry.

1

and guidelines. This has been expanded with the publication of *The UK forestry standard* (Forestry Authority, 1998), setting out criteria and standards for the sustainable management of all forests and woodlands in the UK. It is linked to the Helsinki Guidelines, in which one of the key criteria in sustainable forest management is '...maintenance, conservation and appropriate enhancement of biological diversity in forest ecosystems'.

The UK forestry standard recognises the importance of semi-natural open ground habitats (and by implication, edges), especially where they are extensive or of a diverse or rare type. Both permanent and temporary open space are natural features of most semi-natural woodlands (Plate 1), and are to be encouraged in plantations. In some cases, maintaining open space will require positive intervention through the management of edge vegetation. Restoration or expansion of open space should be based on riparian or wetland zones, parts of the ride network, and landscape or cultural features, across the range of soil types present (Forestry Authority, 1998). Within the general forest design recommendations as part of *The UK forestry standard*, a target of between 10 and 20 % of open space is set, including important edge habitats adjacent to streams, ponds and well-laid-out roads and rides. Where areas are not naturally broken up by topographic features or semi-natural woodland, it may be necessary to create additional open space, designed to develop permanent, structurally diverse internal edges. Note that all specific references to aspects, latitudes and sun altitudes relate to the northern hemisphere.

Aims of this Bulletin:

- To give woodland managers an understanding of the role of edges in forest ecology – Part One, Chapters 2 and 3.

- To enable woodland managers to determine the importance of edges in their situation – Part One, Chapters 4 and 5.

- To provide the management options to maintain and increase the value of edges either for wildlife in general, or for specific species groups – Part Two, Chapters 6, 7, 8 and 9.

Part One

Ecology of Edges and Open Areas

Chapter 2

Ecological value of woodland edges

Edges can be defined as the junction of two different landscape elements such as plant community types, successional stages or land uses (Yahner, 1988), but are seldom defined by a perfectly sharp line (Hunter, 1990). From one set of environmental conditions to another there will always be a transition zone, known as an *ecotone* (Odum, 1971; di Castri *et al.*, 1988).

Edges, ecotones and gaps are *hotspots* for biodiversity in forests. The high diversity of plants and animals associated with edges (Leopold, 1933; Whittaker, 1972) results from the *edge effect*. Ecotone habitats are generally species rich because they support species from the habitats either side of the ecotone, as well as specialised edge species. Furthermore, ecotones are often foci of activity for mobile species as they provide for several needs simultaneously, particularly food and shelter/protection. Good examples of these are grazing and cover for deer, nectar and warm/still conditions for invertebrates, nest/roost sites and foraging areas for many birds. Many species use edges as routes for movement and dispersal.

The edge effect is usually greatest when two adjacent habitats are structurally very different, and hence tend to support different species (Hunter, 1990). The edge effect is most striking between woodland and open habitats (Mitchell and Kirby, 1989). Sometimes the transition is based on an inherent feature of the site. Examples include changes in soil moisture in response to topographical change, altitudinal change creating a shift in microclimate, and a change in the surface geology. These are known as *inherent edges* (Table 2.1), and are long-term, relatively stable features of the landscape. In forests, the presence of marshy ground or rock outcrops, streams or ponds may result in inherent edges.

Induced edges (Table 2.1) are often short-term phenomena created by changes in the vegetation. These exist wherever two different successional stages meet, and can be created by silvicultural operations, as well as by natural disturbance agents such as wind or fire (Hunter, 1990; Angelstam, 1992). Any significant manipulation of the vegetation – planting, felling, fences to exclude grazing animals – can create an induced edge, e.g. along clearfells, roads, rides or linear corridors below powerlines.

Forest edge conditions can extend well into forest stands, particularly where heavy thinning, coppicing or other forms of crown opening occur. *The UK forestry standard* states that the minimum woodland size in order to avoid edge conditions dominating should be 5 hectares. The distinction between edge and interior habitats is often ill-defined and management for forest edge species can involve stand management as much as edge management.

The abundance or proportion of forest edge species has become particularly high in Britain, largely due to the history of deforestation and woodland management. As woods become smaller and more fragmented in the landscape, a larger proportion of their area becomes ecotonal (Harris, 1984). This process has been profound in Britain, where woodlands have long been among the most fragmented in the world (Fuller and Warren, 1991; Spencer and Kirby, 1992). This trend has been further accentuated by traditional coppice and wood-pasture management systems, which also favour edge species (Plate 2). Today's forests therefore tend to be poor in forest interior species and much of the remaining biodiversity in British woodlands, particularly in the lowlands, is adapted to the edge conditions which predominate.

Table 2.1 Factors resulting in ecotones within forests.

	Internal ecotones	External ecotones	Ecological features
Inherent edges	Bogs, wetlands (Plate 4) and water bodies Exposed rock and thin soil Change of soil type	Shoreline Treeline	Decreasing permanence, ⇐ contrast and ecological importance
Induced edges	Roads and rides (Plate 3) Operational open space (loading bays (Plate 5), picnic areas, deer lawns) Firebreaks Wayleaves (Plate 6) Compartment or coupe boundary	Forest land-use boundary Ownership boundary	⇓

Edges and open areas in traditionally managed woodlands

Traditional woodland management practices based on coppicing and wood-pasture have accentuated the importance of forest edge communities in Britain. For example, in managed coppices, gaps are created at the rate of 4–10 % per year, according to tree species and growth rate (Evans, 1984), which is estimated to be a whole order of magnitude greater than the canopy disturbance rate for natural woodlands (Peterken, 1991; Evans and Barkham, 1992). As these silvicultural systems were effective at maintaining edge communities, by periodic opening up of the canopy and ground disturbance, they have an obvious role in perpetuating them, particularly in woodlands which were managed in these ways up to the end of the 19th century (Peterken, 1991). In fact, traditional management tended to maintain unnaturally high populations of many edge species, accentuating the high conservation value of remaining ancient semi-natural woodlands.

In surviving ancient woodland, ride systems are often of considerable antiquity (Peterken, 1991), providing permanent open space habitat networks which are rare in natural woodlands, but none the less particularly species rich (Peterken, 1993) and of great conservation importance (Plate 3).

Edge habitats and open ground in plantation forests

Establishing tree cover, particularly with conifers, results in dramatic reductions in solar radiation influx to the forest floor (Mitchell, 1992; for a review see Mitchell and Kirby, 1989). Following canopy closure, the original semi-natural vegetation and its associated wildlife therefore often becomes restricted to stand edges and remaining open areas (Buckley, 1994), and rides and roadsides take on a particular importance for conservation (Carter and Anderson, 1987; Warren and Fuller, 1993; Buckley et al., 1997a). As well as being important habitats in their own right they provide reservoirs of seeds, plants or animals from which adjacent areas can be colonised after the trees on them have been clearfelled or thinned.

Management activities can create distinctive edge habitats not found elsewhere in the forest, e.g. grassland communities arising on spoil, cuts and ditches from forest road building. While unrepresentative of the forest as a whole these habitats can provide important opportunities for wildlife and can substantially increase habitat diversity in some forests. Grassland communities along forest roads in southern England have become important refugia for some species of flowering plants and butterflies requiring unimproved grassland (Plates 7, 8 and 9; Carter and Anderson, 1987), much of which has been lost due to agricultural intensification (Warren and Fuller, 1993; Sparks and Greatorex-Davies, 1992).

Ecological value of woodland edges: summary

- Edge habitats and open areas within forests are important places for biodiversity.

- The edge effect is most pronounced between woodland and open habitats, and is greatest where edge zones are wide, diverse and permanent.

- Inherent edges are permanent changes in vegetation in response to fixed environmental, climatic, soil or hydrological gradients. Induced edges are temporary changes in vegetation in response to external influences, either natural disturbance events or silvicultural and management impacts.

- Forest edge species are particularly important in British woodlands because historical forest fragmentation and silvicultural regimes based on coppicing and wood pasture favoured edge species and maintained unnaturally high populations which are of conservation importance today.

- Ride systems in ancient woodlands are often of great antiquity and particularly species rich.

- Edge habitats in plantations often form interlinked networks of roads, rides, watercourses, wayleaves, operational open space and stand boundaries which enhance their conservation value. They can serve as sources for recolonisation of felled or thinned stands.

Chapter 3

Light and microclimate

The gradient in microclimate at forest edges produces an environment that is different from, and intermediate between, the open habitat outside the forest and its interior (Angelstam, 1992; Williams-Linera, 1990; Chen *et al.*, 1993). The most influential environmental gradient is solar radiation, which has important implications for the development of understorey vegetation (Anderson, 1979; Beatty, 1984; Hill, 1979), and for the value of edges and gaps to light or heat demanding species.

Solar radiation

Direct radiation, particularly during the growing season (between the spring and autumn equinoxes), is the most appropriate single measure of the light regime at forest edges. The expected direct radiation on rides and in open areas can be calculated from latitude, orientation of open space and tree height (Figure 3.1). A particular point on the ground will be in direct sunlight when the altitude (height) of the tree-tops in the direction of the sun is less than the altitude of the sun itself (i.e. its angle from the horizon). Equations can be used to define the sun's position (Lee, 1978), with variation over time depicted using solar track diagrams. It is also possible to produce *contour maps* to show the sunlight hours across entire clearings at different orientations (Yallop and Hohenkerk, 1991; Figure 3.2).

The microclimate of edges

Canopy removal at forest edges increases direct solar radiation at ground level, and this in combination with reduced wind speeds alters the daily patterns of other microclimatic variables such as air temperature, soil temperature and relative humidity (Chen *et al.*, 1993; Matlack, 1993; Table 3.1). This effect can extend up to three times the canopy height into the forest (Harris, 1984, from studies in boreal forests), or may be much more abrupt (Cadenasso *et al.*, 1997).

Wind speeds tend to be relatively low at forest edges and this results in more extreme air temperatures and humidity. In comparison, air temperature amplitudes are smaller in the forest interior, with lower mean temperatures directly responsible for higher relative humidities. In general, the frequency and amount of dew and frost formation tends to be greatest at the forest edge (Lee, 1978).

Near the edge, greater direct solar radiation tends to dry out the soil surface by evaporation, so during dry periods surface moisture conditions are less favourable for germination (Ranney *et al.*, 1981). At the same time, the regenerating understorey makes added demands for moisture, by the interception of rain and increased transpiration along the forest edge (Ranney *et al.*, 1981). It is possible that, at certain times, this change in soil moisture regime may place an added stress on canopy trees. However soil moisture levels at depth tend to be greater along edges than in the adjacent forest (Lee, 1978) or within clearfelled areas (Chen *et al.*, 1993). Litter decomposition has also been found to be most rapid near edges.

Aspect, slope and latitude

Orientation of edges and open areas has a profound effect on sunlight hours and heat energy received (Carter and Anderson, 1987; Carter, 1991). Wind speed, soil moisture and relative

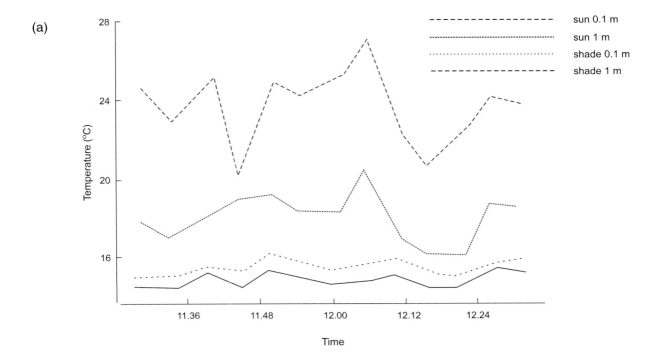

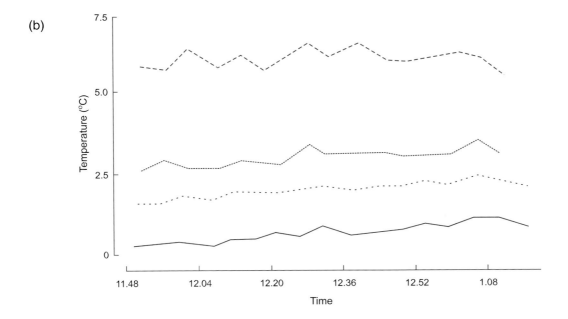

Figure 3.1 Simultaneous air temperature measurements made with shielded thermometers at ground level and 1 m above the ground, in sun and shade, in a 9 m wide E–W oriented forest ride at Holt Pound, Alice Holt Forest, Hampshire on (a) 21 June 1992 and (b) 21 December 1992.

9

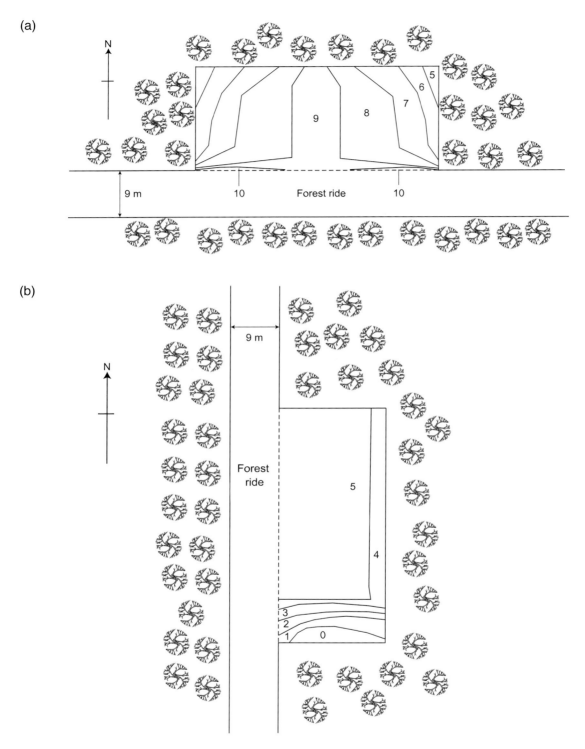

Figure 3.2 Hours of sunlight maps for rideside bays 24 m x 50 m, oriented (a) E–W and (b) N–S, surrounded by trees 15 m tall on 22 June for a latitude of N51° 30'. After Yallop and Hohenkerk (1991).

Table 3.1 The microclimate of edges.

Variable	Edge	Interior
Temperature	Higher and greater diurnal fluctuations	Lower and more stable
Humidity	Lower and greater diurnal fluctuations	Higher and more stable
Dew formation	High	Low
Frost formation	High	Low
Soil moisture deficit near surface	Can be extreme	Rarely extreme
Soil moisture deficit in deeper layers	Less extreme	More extreme
Litter decomposition	Faster	Slower

humidity are also affected. Dramatic differences exist between east–west oriented and north–south oriented clearings (Figures 3.2 and 3.3).

East–west oriented clearings and south-facing edges

In a forest situation, the duration of direct sunlight and daily radiation totals will always be greatest along the south-facing edges of east–west rides as long as clearings have a width equal to, or greater than, the height of the surrounding trees. This so-called 1:1 rule (Carter and Anderson, 1987) applies best in southern Britain and on level ground. Removing trees on the north-facing edge of an east–west ride increases the direct sunlight received by the ride and the south-facing edge (Figure 3.4). In the northern hemisphere, north-facing edges receive direct sunlight only between the spring and autumn equinoxes, and then for only very short periods after sunrise and again prior to sunset (Lee, 1978).

East–west rides accumulate a greater total of direct sunlight hours from the morning (easterly) and evening (westerly) aspects, when the sun is lower and has less heating power. There may be as yet unquantified benefits to certain forms of wildlife from this pattern of sunlight, e.g. increased invertebrate activity around dusk may provide a more suitable foraging environment for woodland bats.

South and west-facing edges experience a higher percentage transmittance of solar radiation into the tree stand than north and east-facing aspects (Patmore, 1990). Removing trees on this south-facing edge, especially where edge trees have particularly deep crowns, greatly increases light penetration into the stand and onto the woodland floor (Figure 3.4).

North–south oriented clearings

If the trees are taller than the ride width, the sun will still fully illuminate north–south oriented rides at midday, when it is potentially at its strongest. Radiation totals are greatest on vertical edges facing toward east or west (i.e. those along clearings oriented north–south) during midsummer days, because the high midday altitude of the sun reduces light transmission into south-facing edges. In areas with mature stands and narrow rides, management of rides oriented north–south might yield greater benefits for wildlife (Figure 3.5).

Effect of latitude and slope

The light regime of the forest and its edge habitats varies with elevation, slope and aspect of the land surface. The lower sun angles at northerly latitudes necessitate further widening of clearings to achieve a light environment comparable with the use of the 1:1 rule in the south (Figure 3.6 and Table 3.2).

South-facing slopes receive greater overall and peak solar radiation than level ground, particularly when open to direct sunlight. Clearings with a southerly aspect are therefore 'hotspots' which are important to the reproductive biology of certain flowering plants and, perhaps more particularly, to the activity of cold-blooded animals. This characteristic has been noted for south-facing banks alongside forest roads (Figure 3.7).

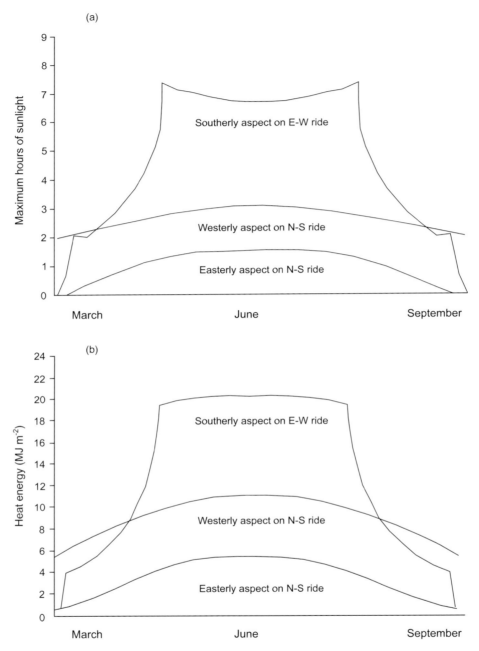

Figure 3.3 Graphs showing (a) maximum hours of sunlight and (b) heat energy for a central point in a hypothetical ride system, widened to equal the height of the trees, for a latitude of N51 30' (Micheldever Forest, Hampshire). After Yallop and Hohenkerk (1991).

At any latitude, greater widening of clearings is required on north-facing slopes to achieve a light environment comparable with the use of the 1:1 rule on level ground. In addition, clearings must be long enough to reduce the shading effect of bay edges, particularly to benefit from morning and evening direct sunlight.

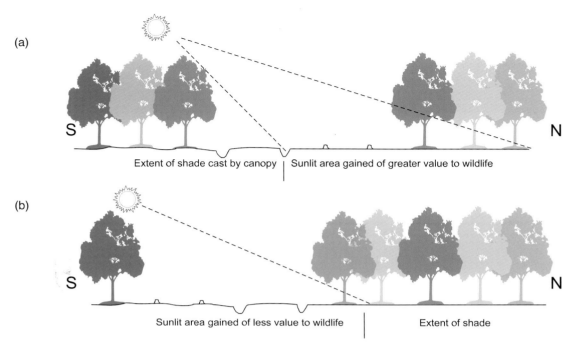

(a)

S   N

Extent of shade cast by canopy | Sunlit area gained of greater value to wildlife

(b)

S   N

Sunlit area gained of less value to wildlife | Extent of shade

Figure 3.4 The effects of removing rows of edge trees (a) from the north edge and (b) from the south edge on the extent of direct sunlight or shade received on a forest ride or road.

N

E

W

S

Shortest shadow axis

Figure 3.5 A ride system for which tree height exceeds ride width on a south-facing slope, under which conditions north–south rides receive greater heat energy as a result of illumination at the middle of the day. East–west rides will accumulate a greater total of sunshine hours from morning and evening illumination, but with less heating power due to lower sun angles.

Table 3.2 Maximum values for sunlight hours received in a 50 m long forest bay alongside a 9 m wide ride.

Latitude and ride orientation	Depth of bay — Crop height																			
	24 m					12 m					9 m					6 m				
	5 m	10 m	15 m	20 m	25 m	5 m	10 m	15 m	20 m	25 m	5 m	10 m	15 m	20 m	25 m	5 m	10 m	15 m	20 m	25 m
57° e.g. Mallaig–Stonehaven																				
E–W	14–15	12–13	10–11	8–9	6–7	14–15	11–12	10–11	8–9	7–8	13–14	11–12	10–11	8–9	7–8	13–14	11–12	10–11	8–9	3–4
N–S	12–13	9–10	6–7	5–6	4–5	10–11	6–7	5–6	4–5	3–4	9–10	5–6	3–4	3–4	2–3	9–10	5–6	3–4	2–3	2–3
54° e.g. Lancaster–York																				
E–W	14–15	12–13	10–11	8–9	7–8	14–15	11–12	10–11	8–9	7–8	13–14	11–12	10–11	8–9	7–8	13–14	11–12	10–11	9–10	4–5
N–S	12–13	9–10	6–7	5–6	4–5	10–11	6–7	4–5	3–4	3–4	9–10	5–6	4–5	3–4	2–3	8–9	5–6	3–4	2–3	2–3
51.5° e.g. Carmarthen–Colchester																				
E–W	13–14	11–12	10–11	8–9	7–8	13–14	11–12	10–11	8–9	7–8	13–14	11–12	10–11	8–9	7–8	12–13	11–12	10–11	8–9	7–8
N–S	12–13	9–10	7–8	5–6	4–5	10–11	6–7	4–5	3–4	3–4	9–10	6–7	4–5	3–4	2–3	8–9	5–6	3–4	2–3	2–3

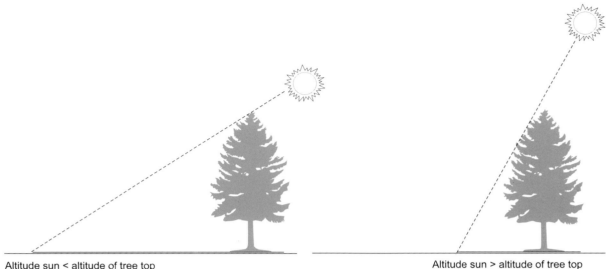

Altitude sun < altitude of tree top
e.g. at higher latitudes where sun angles are reduced

Altitude sun > altitude of tree top
e.g. at lower latitudes

Figure 3.6 The influence of latitude on the relative altitudes of the sun and the tree crop, and hence illumination of the forest floor at woodland edges.

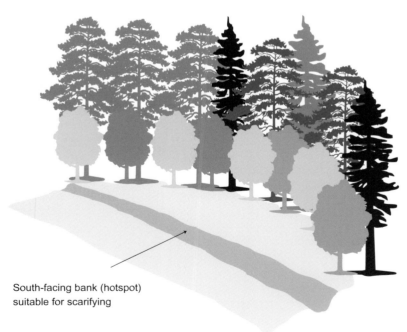

South-facing bank (hotspot)
suitable for scarifying

Figure 3.7 A south-facing road, or rideside bay, showing the 'hotspots' on south-facing banks where the radiation flux is greatest for the period around midday. These may be particularly valuable as reptile basking areas (see Chapter 5) and may be enhanced through scarification to produce bare soil.

Light and microclimate: summary

- Tree cover dramatically reduces light and temperature at ground level, creating an environment unsuitable for many light or heat demanding species. The microclimate also becomes more stable.

- Clearings and rides assume an important conservation role in forests as refugia for heat and light demanding species, particularly where coniferous high forest predominates. The conservation aim should be to maximise direct sunlight into these areas.

- South-facing edges along east–west oriented clearings receive the greatest solar radiation, particularly when on south-facing slopes, as long as the clearing is at least as wide as the crop height. On north-facing slopes east–west rides receive direct sunlight only in the early morning and late afternoon.

- North–south oriented clearings receive direct sunlight at midday. In forests containing narrow clearings in mature stands, north–south clearings may receive most direct sunlight.

- Sun angles are lower at more northerly latitudes and wider clearings are therefore required to achieve a beneficial light environment.

- South- and south-west-facing edges tend to have wide ecotones due to solar radiation and prevailing wind effects.

Chapter 4

Vegetation succession

Manipulation of vegetation succession is the principal management consideration once edges and open areas have been created. Vegetation succession at forest edges can be complex and rapid, partly because of the presence of two or more adjacent plant communities, each in different successional phases (Luken, 1990). Furthermore, the particular expression of vegetation development is affected by various factors:

- regional vegetation types
- successional stage of the forest when an edge is created
- edge aspect
- natural regeneration and herbivore activity
- edge management regimes.

Ecological principles

Secondary succession arises from the recolonisation of a disturbed habitat (Grime, 1979). Typically it appears as a series of changes in species populations, with different species or groups of species successively attaining and then losing dominance (Miles, 1979). Successional changes at forest edges are largely the result of differences in growth and survival rates, competitive ability and longevity between species.

Clearance of woody vegetation (e.g. by cutting-back of rideside edges) is followed by a characteristic process of recolonisation. Annuals, perennial herbs, shrubs and trees are more or less successively represented in the vegetation (Grime, 1979). In most environments, there is no well-defined end-point to succession, and two or more species may coexist in dynamic mixtures.

Succession may be halted by severe forms of disturbance such as burning, grazing, mowing or cultivation resulting in an *arrested succession*. When each form of disturbance is applied repeatedly and consistently, a deflection from the expected succession can result in a distinct *plagioclimax* vegetation type. In forest stands, this can result from repeated selective felling of a particular tree species in a forest, or as a consequence of selective browsing by deer.

Edges influence forest structure and dynamics (Ranney *et al.*, 1981; Figure 4.1). The first stage of development is dominated by the growth of a dense understorey of herbaceous perennials and woody saplings and seedlings. The canopy trees undergo structural changes at a slower rate than that of the understorey, with lateral crown growth toward the increased side lighting at the edge. The second stage of forest edge development is characterised by filling of the space between the canopy and the growing understorey by asymmetrical crown development of individual edge trees. The filling of the edge causes shading (see Chapter 3) and a reduction of wind penetration into the stand which alters the pattern of vegetation invasion and establishment, and leads to the development of a conspicuous edge community. As the stand develops, competition determines which species survive and in what proportions. Eventually, an edge may become dominated by a few larger tree crowns, with the dominant tree species at the edge likely to be different from those in the forest interior.

Regeneration

In a series of monitored edge management trials in lowland plantations in the south of England (Plates 10, 11 and 12), Buckley *et al.* (1997a) found

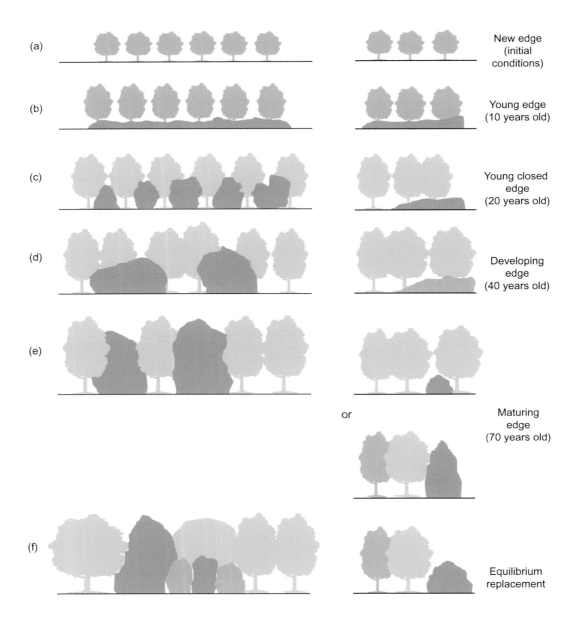

Figure 4.1 (a)-(f): Model for the successional development of vegetation at forest edges. The first stage is dominated by the development of a dense understorey of herbaceous perennials and woody seedlings and saplings. The canopy trees next to the edge respond to the increased side lighting by crown expansion towards the edge, epicormic branching on boles exposed to this increased light, or basal sprouting. Near the edge, the greater incident radiation (heat energy) reduces soil moisture availability, which may place an added stress on canopy trees. At the same time, the newly regenerated understorey makes additional moisture demands through increased interception and evapotranspiration. Precise successional pathways depend upon relative growth rates and adaptations to local conditions of canopy trees and sub-canopy trees and shrubs, eventually reaching an equilibrium replacement phase, at which time greater stability is conferred on the forest edge.

18

that plant species regenerating along newly cut edges occurred in a number of discernible parallel zones (Table 4.1), and that this was occurring within two or three growing seasons. Grasses were typically positioned at the road or ride edges, while annuals, short-lived perennials and ruderals colonised the cut or disturbed zone. Common woodland perennials, including a number of ancient woodland indicator species, maintained stable populations at the new canopy edge or under it (Anderson and Buckley, 1991; Buckley, 1994; Buckley *et al.*, 1997a). Similar findings have been made in Germany (Pietzarka and Roloff, 1993).

Regeneration from seed

Germination from the seedbank is the most rapid form of vegetation development following disturbance during the first or second season after clearance (Brown and Oosterhuis, 1981). Seedbank composition may show little similarity to the groundflora present at the site (Table 4.2).

On alkaline clay soils, initial dominance may be by species such as marsh thistle, hairy St John's wort, and wood spurge, although these generally decline again after four to five years. During this period, they make a colourful display, having the opportunity to flower prolifically, and consequently 'recharging' their seedbanks. In Forestry Commission studies, primrose showed profuse regeneration at some former ancient semi-natural woodland sites previously under 30-year-old beech but were replaced subsequently by perennial grasses and other more stable vegetation. Some species more loosely associated with woodland, such as the grasses, wood millet and wood melick, also possess the capacity for seedbank formation but do not form large and persistent seedbanks, and show only a limited response to edge management (Anderson and Carter, 1987; Buckley *et al.*, 1997b).

Depending upon the woodland type, its history and the surrounding land-use, there are numerous early successional, mainly wind dispersed, plant species which may colonise the site following edge management, such as willowherbs, thistles, foxglove and silver birch. This is accentuated where brash retention delays colonisation from

the seedbank and leads to a flush of nutrient enrichment, favouring species of fertile sites such as common nettle, bramble, thistles and, where the woods are adjacent to agricultural land, edge arable weed species.

Although these species may dominate for a period, their dominance is often transitory and may become replaced by more stable vegetation better reflecting site conditions. This successional loss of, often desirable, species is even more acute for woodland species reliant on vegetative means of regeneration.

Vegetative regeneration

Most specialist woodland plant species (those restricted in their distribution to long-established woodland sites) rely principally upon vegetative means for their regeneration, which in part explains their relatively poor colonising ability. A few (such as bluebell) do produce long-lived seed.

Despite initial increases in cover of dog's mercury following cutting back of the canopy in a series of beech plantations, most woodland species show a decline in response to edge management. Dog's mercury is unable to tolerate the increased sunlight following canopy removal, and may show extensive leaf necrosis (Rackham, 1975). Bluebell may tolerate woodland clearance for a limited period, but yellow archangel shows a rapid decline following canopy removal. True woodland species are therefore rapidly displaced by windblown opportunistic species and others reproducing from buried seed. Grasses such as rough meadow-grass, Yorkshire fog and tufted hair-grass have been found to increase at the expense of species reliant upon vegetative regeneration (Buckley, 1994; Buckley *et al.*, 1997b).

Some species, such as ground ivy, can undergo rapid stoloniferous growth following canopy removal. Similarly, violets respond rapidly to the light by an increase in vegetative growth, thereby providing the essential larval foodplants for fritillary butterflies such as the high brown, silver-washed, pearl-bordered and small pearl-bordered.

Pollination

Insects play an important role at the forest edge. Almost all the colourful flowering plants are

Table 4.1 Representation of the optimum location for different plant species with respect to the gradient between the ride margin and the canopy, using a nine-point preference scale derived from χ^2 frequency testing (after Buckley, 1994).

Ride margin			Cut zone		Canopy edge		Canopy	
a	aab	ab	abb	b	bbc	bc	bcc	c
False oat-grass	Black bent	Lesser burdock	Hazel	Broadleaved willowherb	Enchanter's nightshade	Wood sorrel	Wood anemone	Moschatel
Barren brome	Creeping bent	Silver birch	Rough meadow-grass	Wood spurge	Ivy	Wood meadow-grass	Ash	Common Solomon's seal
	Tufted hair-grass	False wood brome	Wood dock	Wood millet	Three-veined sandwort		Bluebell	
	Wild strawberry	Wood sedge	Wood speedwell	Common dog-violet	Lesser celandine		Yellow archangel	
	Cleavers	Creeping thistle					Dog's mercury	
	Herb Robert	Marsh thistle						
	Ground ivy	Rosebay willowherb						
	Hogweed	Creeping soft-grass						
	Yorkshire fog	Hairy St John's wort						
	Trailing St John's wort	Perforated St John's wort						
	Hedge woundwort	Soft rush						
		Common rush						
		Bramble						
		Broadleaved dock						
		Common nettle						

0	1	2	3	4	5	6	7	8	9	10	11	12	13	14	15	16	17	18	19	20

Approximate distance along transect (metres)

a: ride margin; b: cut zone; c: canopy edge/canopy. Single letters indicate exclusivity, i.e. species occurring only in one particular zone; two identical letters indicate a preference for a particular zone, but no restriction to it; two different letters only occurring together indicate no preference for either zone.

For list of scientific names, see Appendix 2.

Table 4.2 Vascular plant species composition above ground and in the soil seedbank for a chronosequence of Norway spruce, Forest of Dean, Gloucestershire.

Plant species	Pre-thicket			Mid-rotation			Mature		
	Above ground	Soil seedbank	Both	Above ground	Soil seedbank	Both	Above ground	Soil seedbank	Both
Sweet vernal-grass	✔						✔		
Rough meadow-grass		✔							
Wood meadow-grass		✔			✔			✔	
False brome	✔			✔					
Common bent-grass	✔	✔	✔	✔	✔	✔	✔		
Creeping bent-grass		✔			✔				
Yorkshire fog		✔							
Creeping soft-grass							✔		
Red fescue		✔			✔			✔	
Sheep's fescue					✔				
Tall fescue		✔							
Wavy hair-grass							✔	✔	✔
Tufted hair-grass	✔	✔	✔		✔				
Wood sedge						✔	✔	✔	✔
Foxglove	✔	✔	✔		✔		✔	✔	✔
Wood sorrel	✔	✔	✔		✔		✔		
Bracken	✔			✔			✔		
Wild strawberry	✔								
Perforate St John's wort	✔	✔	✔						
Slender St John's wort		✔							
Rosebay willowherb		✔					✔	✔	✔
Pale willowherb	✔								
Spear-leaved willowherb								✔	
Creeping buttercup	✔								
Bramble	✔	✔	✔	✔	✔	✔	✔		
Bluebell		✔			✔				
Black medick	✔						✔		
Yellow pimpernel	✔								
Heath bedstraw									
Hedge bedstraw	✔								
Greater stitchwort	✔								
Common nettle	✔	✔	✔		✔				
Cuckooflower		✔							
Knotgrass							✔		
Common dog-violet	✔								
Dandelion	✔								
Ivy	✔						✔		
Lady-fern				✔					
Broad buckler-fern				✔			✔		
Male-fern				✔			✔		
Norway spruce							✔		
Pedunculate oak	✔						✔		
Hawthorn	✔								
Holly	✔						✔		
Silver birch		✔					✔		
Rowan							✔		
Sweet chestnut							✔		
Douglas fir							✔		
Beech							✔		
Gorse							✔		
Hybrid larch							✔		

dependent upon insects for pollination and the production of fertile seeds. Apart from being propagules for the continued survival of the plant species, these seeds, berries and fruits are major components in the diet of both resident and migratory birds, notably the finches and thrushes (see Chapter 5). In addition to the various nectar and pollen gathering bees, there are other generalist insect pollinators, some being particularly associated with certain plant families. There are also some species that more or less confine their food gathering to particular species of flowers (see Table 4.3).

Table 4.3 Examples of mining bees, pollinating insects that largely confine their nectar and pollen gathering to particular flowering plants (based on Müller, 1883 and Chinery, 1986).

Mining bee species	Flowering plant
Andrena florea	White bryony
Andrena fulva	Currants
Andrena hattorfiana	Field scabious
Andrena labiata	Speedwell
Andrena pallipes	Dandelion
Anthophora plumipes	Lungwort
Chelostoma campanularum	Bellflowers
Chelostoma florisomne	Buttercups
Macropis labiata	Yellow loosestrife

Impact of herbivores

Edge management creates vegetation communities attractive to a range of herbivores. Their impact can be great when at high density or where open ground and regenerating woody vegetation is scarce. Herbivores can be classified into grazers, which are adapted to feed on grasses, or browsers which mainly feed on leaves, twigs, buds and herbaceous plants (Table 4.4). The species present in Britain can be ranked in the following sequence from browser to grazer: muntjac, roe deer, goat, red deer, sika deer, fallow deer, rabbit, sheep, horse and cattle. In general, larger animals are less selective than smaller animals and browsers are

more selective than grazers. The impact of muntjac and roe deer, which focus on trees and herbs and avoid grasses, is therefore noticeably very different from that of cattle which reduce the height of grassy vegetation.

In many areas it is deer that will have the greatest impact on edge and open space vegetation communities. For example, red deer have been reported to have a noticeable effect on vegetation at densities below 4 km^{-2}, and regeneration can fail completely at 25 km^{-2} or more. Some studies have shown that roe and fallow can achieve higher densities (up to 10 km^{-2}) before similar effects become apparent. The increasing scarcity of aspen in some localities is thought to be attributable to it being particularly palatable to red deer, roe deer and cattle (Carter, 1991).

Shrub and tree regeneration

Herbivores have a fundamental impact on tree and shrub regeneration in most British woodlands and may jeopardise management to improve the structural diversity of woodland edges. The impact grazing animals have will usually increase as their numbers rise. At low densities the size or number of the most susceptible species is reduced. As densities increase this effect is transferred to the less palatable species and the most palatable are eliminated altogether. At this stage, one or two of the most resistant species will actually increase in number. At the highest densities, tree regeneration will be prevented altogether. This is a common consequence wherever domestic animals are allowed to graze in British woodlands.

Thornber (1993), studying vegetation structure and composition in a series of fenced exclosure plots along five-year-old ride edges in lowland beech plantation, found highly significant differences in vegetation height and composition of woody species between fenced and unfenced areas (Figure 4.2 and Plate 12). Although seedling recruitment was similar in both areas, heavy browsing by roe deer and hares in unfenced areas led to almost total elimination of woody saplings and tall herbs. Many of these early successional species can be expected to recover, provided browsing pressure is reduced, since they are

Table 4.4 The vegetation impact of mammalian herbivores (Gill, 1991).

	Diet	Examples of impact
Cattle	Selective grazer	Creation of shrub dominated communities under heavy grazing or in nutrient poor sites.
Horses	Coarse grazer	Remove species (e.g. rushes, reeds and thistles) usually avoided by cattle and sheep. Can graze wetter areas and poorer quality forage than cattle.
Sheep	Very selective grazer	Create mosaic of short and tall pastures. Some species (e.g. bracken and rushes) conspicuously avoided.
Goats	Browser/grazer	Reduce shrub biomass. Consume grasses in spring.
Rabbits	Grazer	Maintain short lawns close to burrow systems. Patchy effect.
Red deer	Intermediate browser/grazer	Selective removal of tree species. All tree regeneration prevented at moderate densities.
Roe deer	Selective browser	Suppression of some dicotyledonous species (e.g. rosebay willowherb). Alteration to tree species composition. Removal of coppice regrowth.
Fallow deer	Intermediate browser/grazer	Suppression of tree regeneration (both broadleaves and conifers) and depletion of herbs and shrubs. Bark stripping and fraying of young trees and saplings.
Muntjac	Selective browser	Suppression or removal of broadleaved (not conifer) tree regeneration and coppice regrowth. Herbs and shrubs (e.g. honeysuckle, bluebells, ivy) depleted.

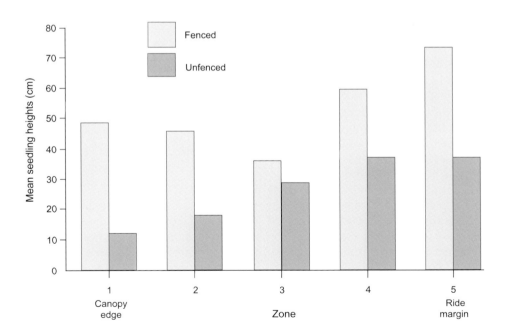

Figure 4.2 Mean seedling heights of regenerating trees and shrubs on a newly created ride edge, five years after cutting back of the tree canopy, showing the impact of protection from herbivore browsing using fenced exclosures, Micheldever Forest, Hampshire (P31-35 beech). Data from Thornber (1993).

Table 4.5 Susceptibility of tree species to deer damage.

Browsing on broadleaves	willows > ash > oak > rowan > Norway maple > sycamore > beech > lime > hornbeam > birch > alder
Bark stripping	willows > ash > rowan > aspen > lodgepole pine > beech > Norway spruce > Scots pine > larch > Douglas fir > Sitka spruce > silver fir > oak > alder > birch
Browsing on conifers	silver fir > Douglas fir > Norway spruce > Scots pine > Sitka spruce > lodgepole pine > Corsican pine

known to respond to browsing by replacing lost tissue through compensatory growth (Bryant *et al.*, 1983).

Where some form of cyclic linear coppicing is practised along roadsides and ride edges, high deer populations prevent regeneration from the cut stools. This will promote open sunny conditions but will result in an abrupt boundary between the tree stand and open space. The suppression of scrub growth will also reduce the diversity of shrub species as foodplants or for nesting cover. Foliar cover of bramble, a highly palatable species, can be significantly reduced by browsing (Grime *et al.*, 1988), but its removal may be favourable for the development of a more diverse groundflora (Gill, 1991a; Thomas and Kirby, 1992).

The relative preferences for browsing and bark stripping of woody species (Table 4.5) have been compiled from various sources (Mitchell *et al.*, 1977; Gill, 1991b) and should be taken as a general guide only, considering that other factors can also affect damage. In view of the fact that broadleaves are usually browsed in the summer and conifers in the winter, browsing preferences of these two groups have been listed separately. Preferential browsing can have a major effect on the species composition of woody regeneration. Oak is often replaced by less palatable sycamore in the presence of low herbivore densities. However, where herbivores are completely excluded, ash and birch seedlings are sometimes initially abundant but cannot compete well with grasses or brambles, which become more prolific after fencing.

The use of individual tree protection to protect woody regeneration is generally prohibitively expensive and difficult with coppice regrowth. Only where browsing pressure is severe and the conservation of particular tree or shrub species is a priority, such as nature reserves or SSSIs, may protection be considered. Control of deer numbers or ranging behaviour, rather than total exclusion, may be required to allow the desired vegetation structure to develop (see Chapter 8), particularly considering the wider impacts of herbivores on field and ground layer vegetation.

Field and ground vegetation

In forest habitats, most herbivores concentrate their feeding in rides or openings. Their impact on field and ground vegetation may not be immediately noticeable, but can have an important effect upon the relative abundance of species in the ground and field layers. The most conspicuous effect of grazing is the reduction in vegetation height or above ground biomass. This also reduces the amount of dead plant material, increases the rate of nutrient cycling, improves light transmission and reduces average plant size. Grazing animals usually also remove taller or faster growing dominants, giving smaller, slower growing plants an opportunity to reproduce. Some rare plants can disappear altogether if grazing animals are excluded from woodland.

Under light to moderate grazing floristic diversity is increased, not simply because light transmission is improved and mean tree size reduced, but because faster growing dominants are removed and smaller slower growing but grazing-tolerant species are able to compete. The density of herbivores required to maximise diversity of ground-layer plants is much greater than that for acceptable tree survival.

Mosses, bracken and grasses usually all benefit from grazing, whether by sheep or deer. Some

Table 4.6 Impact of excluding herbivores on changes in abundance of plant species following ride widening treatments in woodlands in Hampshire, England (from Buckley et al., 1997a).

Species that increased in unfenced controls	Duration of increase (maximum 4 years)	Species that increased in fenced exclosures	Duration of increase (maximum 4 years)
Grasses			
Creeping bent	1–2	Creeping bent	1
False wood-brome	2–3	False oat-grass	1
Yorkshire fog	1–2	False wood-brome	1
		Cocksfoot	1
		Tufted hair-grass	1–3
		Wood millet	1
		Rough meadow-grass	1
Herbs			
Wood rush	1–2	Wood rush	1
Enchanter's nightshade	1	Traveller's joy	2
Creeping thistle	1	Rosebay willowherb	1–3
Marsh thistle	1	Broadleaved willowherb	1–2
Foxglove	1	Square-stalked willowherb	1
Narrow buckler-fern	1	Wild strawberry	1
Broadleaved willowherb	1	Hairy St John's wort	1
Cleavers	1	Yellow archangel	1–2
Ivy	2	Honeysuckle	1
Hairy St John's wort	1–2	Dog's mercury	1
Dog's mercury	2	Creeping buttercup	1
Broadleaved dock	1	Clustered dock	1
Common nettle	1	Common ragwort	1
		Germander speedwell	1
Woody species			
Hazel	1	Beech	1
		Ash	1–4
		Bramble	1–2

other unpalatable species, like foxgloves, ragwort and ground ivy have also been found to increase. Deer browsing can cause a conspicuous reduction in some herbaceous plants like rosebay willowherb, ivy and bramble which are staple food plants. In ride management trials in southern England, perforate St John's wort became one of the dominant field layer herbs in the presence of grazing, and is known to contain a latex and hypericin, a chemical defence against herbivory (Cooper and Johnson, 1984). On some heavier soils, the local dominance of tufted hair-grass may be exacerbated as a result of its avoidance by herbivores, the coarse leaves having a high silica content (Grime et al., 1988). At experimental sites in woodlands in Hampshire some areas were fenced and others left unfenced after ride widening (Buckley et al., 1997a). The effect on field layer species is summarised in Table 4.6. However, such data must be treated as no more than indicative since herbivore species and composition of available forage have a strong influence (Gill, 1991a).

Rabbits and hares may selectively remove some species, maintaining short, often grass-dominated swards. With their distinct dunging behaviour, the vegetation may develop a patchy distribution pattern (Gill, 1991a). Open grassy areas such as widened rides and roadsides provide suitable habitat and corridors for a range of small mammals, especially field voles and, where cover is greater, bank voles and wood mice (Gurnell, 1985). High numbers of voles can also be considerably destructive in selectively browsing regenerating plants in the winter months. Invertebrate herbivory at forest and woodland edges also occurs, but it is less predictable or understood than vertebrate herbivory.

Vegetation succession: summary

- Manipulation of vegetation succession is the principal consideration of management once edges and open areas have been created.
- After clearance of woody vegetation a characteristic process of recolonisation takes place with annuals, perennial herbs, shrubs and trees successively represented in the vegetation.
- As vegetation succession proceeds plant species diversity can decline and many desirable species may be lost.
- Plant species at forest edges occur in a number of discernible parallel zones. Grasses are typically positioned at road or ride edges, with annuals, short-lived perennials and ruderals in the disturbed zone, and common woodland perennials maintaining stable populations at or beneath the canopy edge.
- Germination from the soil seedbank is the most rapid form of vegetation development following disturbance, and tends to be most pronounced where complete canopy and brash clearance occurs.
- Woodland species show only a limited response to edge management, relying on vegetative means of regeneration and having relatively poor colonising ability. They are soon outcompeted and replaced by other species along open, well-lit edges.
- The activity of woodland herbivores is often concentrated at edges and open spaces within forests, and may jeopardise management to improve edge diversity.
- Light to moderate grazing generally increases floristic, structural and spatial diversity of ground vegetation.
- The grazing level required to maximise plant species diversity is generally greater than the maximum level to achieve woody regeneration.
- Complete exclusion of herbivores eventually results in rank and dense vegetation dominated by a few competitive species.

Chapter 5

Animals in woodland edges and open areas

Woodland managers are often interested in edge vegetation because of its value as habitat for the animals and plant communities they wish to conserve. The ecological value of ecotones between woodland and adjacent open areas is well known, and these edge habitats are recognised as areas of intensive use by wildlife (Ranney *et al.*, 1981).

Well-developed woodland edges which are structurally diverse are likely to provide suitable niches for numerous animal species. This effect will be greatest where the edge zones contrast markedly with the adjacent woodland stand. Consequently, rides, glades, roadsides, riparian zones and external edges may be concentrations of wildlife. This is the case in many conifer dominated plantation forests. For many vertebrate species, vegetation structure is generally more important than composition in determining habitat quality (Ferris-Kaan and Patterson, 1992).

However, the actual species composition of the plant communities is also important, particularly to phytophagous species. For example, many butterflies are very specific in terms of their larval foodplant selection, down to both plant species and individuals; a common phenomenon is the selection of large, conspicuous individual plants in the general vegetation (Porter, 1993). The attractiveness of woodland edges to many resident bird species may be in part determined by the presence of shrubs bearing winter berries (Snow and Snow, 1988), while foraging bats will favour edges composed of native broadleaved trees and shrubs such as birch, willow and cherry (wild and bird) which are especially important as foodplants for many species of nocturnally active moths (Plate 13; Mayle and Gurnell, 1991).

It is possible that linear landscape features between habitat patches provide corridors for some wildlife. Forest rides and roadsides may function in this way. Firm evidence of such a corridor function in British forests is hard to find (Kirby, 1995), although anecdotal evidence suggests that small mammals may utilise grassy rides in this way (Gurnell, 1985). A few notable exceptions are butterflies such as the heath fritillary which is able to migrate and colonise new areas of suitable habitat within woodland, through the provision of interconnected ride networks (Warren, 1987a and b). However, given the often dramatic changes associated with the afforestation of former open ground, there is a generally held view that networks of open space are beneficial, at least for some more mobile taxonomic groups.

Fragmentation of both heathland and grassland habitats may to some extent be ameliorated through the creation or restoration of linkages between patches of open ground. The structure and width of heathland rides is important to the dispersal of target species. For example, Dent and Spellerberg (1987) suggest that lizards (common and sand) require a minimum mean width of 5.6 m between the ride edge and the plantation trees.

Invertebrates

Open, sunny rides, glades and roadsides are of considerable importance to invertebrates that exploit the early stages of woodland succession (Plates 14 and 15). Most invertebrates have annual life-cycles and need suitable breeding conditions every year if populations are to survive, and they frequently have completely different requirements at different stages of their life-cycles (Warren and Fuller, 1993).

In order to meet the many, often contrasting, needs of a diverse range of invertebrate species, it is usually advisable to undertake a general management programme, designed to create diverse edge habitats. Exceptions to this concern locally or nationally rare species, whose needs may take precedent over other more common species. Woodland nature reserves and SSSIs may require management for particular species, e.g. vegetation management to favour violets for pearl-bordered fritillaries (Plates 8 and 9(b); Greatorex-Davies et al., 1992).

Requirements of woodland and woodland edge species

It is important to distinguish between the habitat needs of woodland and woodland edge species and species of the open habitats (e.g. grassland and heathland) contained within forests. The relative value of open and early seral woodland habitats will often depend on the legacy of invertebrate biodiversity remaining from historical and adjacent land use. Where rides and glades contain remnants of unimproved grassland, a range of invertebrates may be supported which are not normally associated with woodland (Steel and Khan, 1986). These open habitats have sometimes become important remnants protected from agricultural improvement and can be nationally significant for scarce grassland or heathland species. In contrast, where the woodland has become established on a site formerly managed as coppice, many of the invertebrates are those adapted to the cyclic provision of open ground under a traditional coppice regime (Fuller and Warren, 1993; Greatorex-Davies, 1991) and their habitat needs are often quite distinct from those associates of grassland and heathland. Sites historically managed as high forest or wood pasture have a different species complement again.

Flowering plants for invertebrates

The general management approach is to provide the open, sunny conditions in which flowering plants will thrive, simply by cutting back the stand edge and allowing vegetation succession to proceed, irrespective of the seedbank present. This often results, for several years at least, in an assemblage of flowering plants which attracts insects of many groups. The flowers of Compositae and Umbelliferae which often predominate are highly attractive to insects (Table 5.1). The form of the flowers in the Compositae is more useful to insects with long tongues, i.e. bees, butterflies and moths. The flowers of the Umbelliferae have their nectar secreted on an open disc and have easily accessible pollen, and this tends to be favoured by insects with shorter mouthparts, i.e. flies, parasitic hymenoptera and beetles (see Table 5.1). Bumble bees show a marked preference for the larger flowers found in the families Scrophulariaceae (e.g. great mullein, foxglove) and Labiatae (e.g. bugle, white dead-nettle). These nectar and pollen feeders, in turn, attract predators such as dragonflies and damselflies, which will often hunt along rides and roadsides in search of insect prey (Warren and Fuller, 1993).

Encouraging butterflies and moths

Much edge and open space management has focused on promotion of habitats suitable for butterflies and moths, e.g. at Bernwood Forest, Oxfordshire. In studies carried out in a series of beech plantations in southern England, the creation of new woodland rides by clearfelling in 20-metre wide strips (to equal the height of the trees at the time of felling; Plates 10 and 11), led to a dramatic increase in the total numbers of individuals and species of butterfly in the first 2-3 years after felling (Carter, 1991; Figure 5.1). Much is known about the preferred adult and larval foodplants for butterflies (Table 5.2), and minimum breeding areas have been estimated (Table 5.3).

In addition to the grass and herb vegetation, trees and shrubs along woodland edges can be important for butterflies and particularly moths (Plate 13). The purple emperor breeds on sallows growing in sheltered ride and roadside margins and depends upon open rides for its courtship and territorial flight (Wilmott, personal communication). The silver-washed fritillary tends to breed in dappled shade beneath the woodland canopy, but prefers sunny glades, rides and other edges when not egg-laying (Thomas, 1989; Warren and Fuller, 1993). Although the decline of woodland

Table 5.1 Records of insects visiting flowers of some of the more common species of composites and umbellifers (after Müller, 1883).

	Total number of species observed to visit the flowers	Proportion of species (%) in each insect group			
		Lepidoptera (butterflies and moths)	Apidae (bees)	Diptera (flies)	Other insects
Compositae					
Dandelion	93	7.5	62.5	22.6	7.4
Creeping thistle	88	7.9	36.4	27.3	28.4
Yarrow	87	6.9	34.5	24.1	34.5
Ox-eye daisy	72	6.9	16.6	38.9	37.5
Brown knapweed	48	27	58.7	12.5	2
Welted thistle	44	9.1	72.7	6.8	11.3
Ragwort	40	7.5	40	45	7.5
Hawkweed ox-tongue	29	10.3	55.2	31	3.4
Tansy	27	18.5	25.9	25.9	29.6
Hemp agrimony	18	50	11.1	33.3	5.5
Mean	–	15.2	41.4	26.7	16.7
Umbelliferae					
Hogweed	118	0	11	41.5	47.4
Ground elder	104	0	14.4	32.6	52.9
Cow parsley	73	0	6.8	35.6	57.5
Wild carrot	61	3.3	13.1	31.1	52.5
Caraway	55	1.8	16.4	38.2	43.6
Dill	46	0	13	32.6	54.3
Water parsnip	32	0	0	62.5	37.5
Wild angelica	30	3.3	6.6	36.6	53.3
Rough chervil	23	0	4.3	43.5	52.2
Burnet saxifrage	23	0	13	34.8	52.2
Mean	–	0.8	9.9	38.9	50.4

fritillaries has coincided with the general reduction of coppicing, the white admiral, which uses honeysuckle growing in woodland shade for egg laying and as a larval foodplant, has extended its range (Pollard, 1979). Apart from the variety of foodplants for the larvae of many species of moths that occur along woodland edges, it is the shelter brought about by the vegetation and the residual warmth from daytime sun that entices the adult moths to forage for nectar.

The shrubby margins of rides are of vital importance to moths, especially in conifer plantations where broadleaved trees may be otherwise scarce. Sallows and aspen are particularly important ride and roadside trees for insects of many different orders. Other trees and shrubs that grow in these situations including blackthorn, wayfaring-tree, guelder-rose, buckthorn, wild privet, spindle and field maple have host-plant-specific moths (Warren and Fuller, 1993).

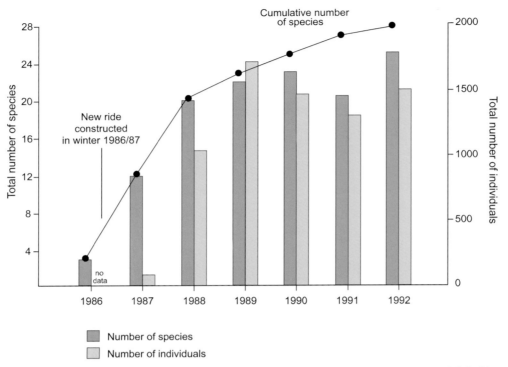

Figure 5.1 Butterfly responses to ride management in a P31-36 beech plantation 1986-1991, Micheldever Forest, Hampshire.

Management to maximise invertebrate diversity

Positive action to control the light conditions in woodland rides and other open areas by vegetation management is vital for the maintenance of high invertebrate diversity. Attempts have been made to calculate the light conditions which best suit particular species or groups (Warren, 1985; Hall and Greatorex-Davies, 1989; Warren and Fuller, 1993; Sparks and Greatorex-Davies, 1992). Generally, the majority of invertebrate species require very open sunny rides, although a few butterfly species such as the wood white and ringlet (Plate 15) prefer partially shaded conditions (10–40 % shade) (Greatorex-Davies, 1991). The speckled wood and green-veined white prefer fairly well-shaded rides with 40–90 % shade. This approach can be applied to other invertebrate groups utilising woodland edge habitats, e.g. Heteroptera, Coleoptera, Chrysomelidae and Curculionidae; and it allows predictions to be made concerning the effect of increasing shade on their populations (Sparks and Greatorex-Davies, 1992; Greatorex-Davies et al., 1994; Sparks et al., 1996).

Woodland edges can provide a range of suitable habitats for invertebrates and, in addition to straightforward ride widening, sheltered bays, scallops and 'box-junctions' can be particularly valuable (Plate 16). Often this value is a result of their being relatively more sheltered, with a warmer microclimate (Steel and Khan, 1986). They also increase the area of grassy verge habitat and, being of greater dimensions than conventional edges, allow for more intricate management to be carried out, involving cutting individual segments according to different regimes and cycles (Figure 5.2).

Management to promote specific species or groups may require more subtle intervention based on an understanding of their habitat requirements. For example, many species of bees and wasps need patches of bare ground in which

Table 5.2 Popular adult nectar sources (a) and larval foodplants (b) for butterflies found in woodland.

(a)

Nectar foodplants	Flowering seasons
Primrose	Mar–Jun
Sallow	Mar–Apr
Bluebell	Apr–Jun
Bugle	Apr–Jun
Lady's smock	Apr–Jun
Ragged robin	May–Aug
Bramble	May–Sep
Bird's-foot trefoil	May–Sep
Tufted vetch	May–Sep
Betony	Jun–July
Wild privet	Jun–Sep
Tormentil	Jun–Aug
Valerian	Jun–Oct
Ragwort	Jun–Oct
Devil's-bit scabious	July–Sep
Heather	July–Oct
Knapweeds	July–Sep
Hemp agrimony	July–Sep
Fleabane	Aug–Sep

(b)

Larval foodplants	
Grasses e.g. Yorkshire fog, fescues, timothy	Spindle
	Broom
Violets	Gorse
Devil's bit-scabious	Buckthorn
Common cow-wheat	Blackthorn
Ribwort plantain	Bird's-foot trefoil
Stinging nettle	Greater bird's-foot trefoil
Sallow	Meadow vetchling
Honeysuckle	Bitter vetch
Cowslip	Common stork's-bill
Primrose	Wild strawberry
Holly	Creeping cinquefoil
Ivy	Lady's smock
Dogwood	Garlic mustard

to burrow for nests. South-facing dry road or rideside banks, which develop a suitably warm microclimate, are particularly valuable (Warren and Fuller, 1993); the tipped-up root plates of wind-blown trees can also be colonised by these insects. Tall vegetation or scrub is used by some spiders and many plant-feeding invertebrates, which in turn support a range of other invertebrate predators and parasites, as well as providing food for larger animals such as birds. Predatory species vary in the specificity of their requirements. For example, four common species of ground-dwelling wolf spiders were found to be significantly more abundant in pitfall traps on the south-facing aspect compared with the north-facing aspect of an east–west ride (Table 5.4). The south-facing edge had the possibility of 10 hours continuous sunshine compared with two $1^{1}/_{2}$ hour periods on the north-facing edge. In contrast, six common species of ground beetles showed no difference in numbers trapped between aspect, possibly on account of their tendency to be nocturnally active.

Birds

The width and structure of edges have the greatest influence on their value for birds. In general, narrow clearings and those with no marginal belt of shrubby vegetation are of least value (Warren and Fuller, 1993) and little used for nesting (Fuller, 1991; Fuller and Whittington, 1987; Gates and Gysel, 1978). Very few bird species actually feed on the open surface of rides, glades and roadside verges, although blackbirds, song thrushes and robins nesting in the adjacent woodland frequently do (Warren and Fuller, 1993). Raptors such as sparrowhawks may hunt for small birds along woodland edges.

Scrub management
The presence of a substantial scrubby margin is essential (Plate 13) and, although detailed prescriptions do not exist, it is likely that these strips should be at least 5 m wide in order to have maximum value (Fuller, 1991). In addition, the density of vegetation at the base of this scrub margin is known to be of importance to some species (Clements and Tofts, 1992).

Table 5.3 The population structure of UK butterflies and the minimum area from which a viable colony has been recorded (after Thomas, 1984).

Closed populations						Unknown area populations	Open or migratory populations
Minimum breeding area							
0.5–1 ha	1–2 ha	2–5 ha	5–10 ha	10–50 ha	> 50 ha		
Essex skipper	Lulworth skipper	Marsh fritillary	Small pearl-bordered fritillary	Swallowtail	Purple emperor	Chequered skipper	Holly blue
Small skipper	Dingy skipper	Glanville fritillary	Pearl-bordered fritillary	Brown hairstreak		Northern brown argus	Comma
Silver-spotted skipper	Grizzled skipper			Large copper		Dark green fritillary	Orange tip
Large skipper	Wood white			White admiral		High brown fritillary	Green-veined white
Purple hairstreak	Green hairstreak					Silver-washed fritillary	Small white
Black hairstreak	Small copper					Speckled wood	Large white
White-letter hairstreak	Brown argus					Wall brown	Small tortoiseshell
Small blue	Common blue					Mountain ringlet	Peacock
Silver-studded blue	Adonis blue					Scotch argus	Large tortoiseshell
Chalkhill blue	Large blue					Large heath	Red admiral
Large blue	Grayling					Gatekeeper	Painted lady
Duke of Burgundy fritillary						Ringlet	Clouded yellow
Heath fritillary							
Small heath							
Meadow brown							
Marbled white							
Total 15	11	2	2	4	1	12	12

The majority of British butterflies live in discrete colonies which breed in the same small areas, close by, year after year. Colonies typically fluctuate considerably in size, ranging from under 50 adults in a poor season to a few hundred in a good one. Other species are much more mobile, and disperse widely, laying eggs wherever suitable conditions are found. There are a few butterflies that regularly migrate to Britain, e.g. the red admiral, painted lady and clouded yellow (details from Thomas, 1989).

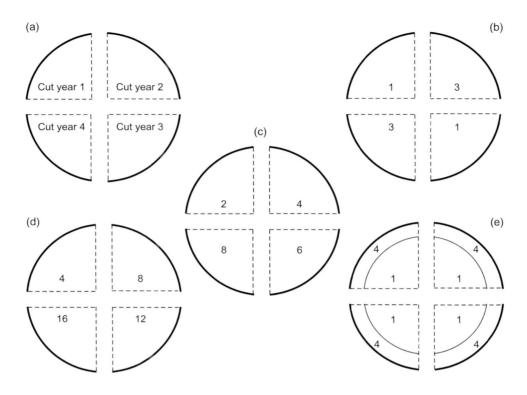

Figure 5.2 Cutting regimes for box junctions at forest road or ride intersections (after Steel and Khan, 1986).

Management involving the cutting back of ride or roadside edges and the creation of marginal strips of scrubby vegetation may potentially benefit a range of bird species (Fuller, 1991). Most of the woodland warblers occurring in Britain can respond positively to this form of management, with chiff-chaffs strongly associated with low, tangled vegetation along rides and the edges of glades in some woods (Fuller, 1991; Warren and Fuller, 1993). Other summer visitors, such as the nightingale, will nest in the shrubby margins of woodland edges. Scandinavian research has demonstrated an edge effect for tree-gleaning species such as chaffinch and various species of tit (Hansson, 1983).

Insectivorous species

Insects are the primary source of food for summer migratory birds. The peak flowering time of sallow along forest rides appears to coincide with the early arrival of willow warblers and chiffchaffs that feed on insects attracted to the flowering

sallows. Caterpillars of the moths in the family Lasiocampidae (feeding on a range of broadleaved trees and shrubs such as blackthorn, hawthorn, sallow and bramble) that emerge in spring to complete their development are the favoured food of newly arrived cuckoos. Later in the year, it is the lepidopterous caterpillars from trees and other plants that form the rich food for the developing nestlings of woodland birds. Open sunny sheltered rides and woodland edges are also essential for ants and large wood ants to thrive, which in turn are the favoured food of the green woodpecker and other insectivorous birds.

Gamebirds

The management of external woodland edges and rides for gamebirds, particularly pheasants, has received much attention (Woodburn, 1991; Robertson, 1992). It is now well known that the management of edges is critical in maximising the density of pheasants within a woodland, and that rides should be greater than 30 m in width to be

Table 5.4 A comparison of the number of wolf spiders and ground beetles collected in pitfall traps sited in opposing aspects along an east–west ride edge in 50-year-old beechwood, Micheldever, Hampshire.

	3/3[a]	16/3[a]	31/3[a]	14/4[a]	28/4	11/5	27/5	20/6	28/7	Total
					Date					
Spiders										
North aspect	0	5	2	8	6	21	10	2	4	58
South aspect	1	1	2	13	27	121	146	22	14	347
Ground beetles										
North aspect	0	1	2	7	28	58	69	69	69	397
South aspect	0	4	6	7	14	69	46	64	151	361

[a]These sample dates are before the tree canopy has come into leaf.

beneficial (Plate 17; Woodburn, 1991). The factors which appear to influence the density of birds in a wood are the length of edge and the extent of shrub cover within this zone.

Management prescriptions

Detailed edge management prescriptions for birds still need to be determined, but Warren and Fuller (1993) propose that the cutting of linear coppice belts of 10–20 m width on either side of rides or roads may be one option that could favour migrant birds. Such strips of coppice are of greatest value for breeding when dense and between 6–8 years old (Currie, 1991). Coppice cutting operations are best carried out during the winter, when the trees are dormant and when there is no danger of disturbance to nesting birds.

Mammals

Woodland edge grassland and shrubby vegetation can support large populations of small mammals, the composition being dependent upon the stage of vegetation succession and structural development. Although edge management is unlikely to affect mammal species richness, the distribution, persistence and relative abundance of mammal communities will change (Mayle and Gurnell, 1991).

Vegetation cover and predation

The edge management regime adopted influences vegetation cover and the ease of predation. For example, close cutting of rideside vegetation increases the vulnerability of small mammals to predation while leaving vegetation to grow longer decreases vulnerability (Mayle and Gurnell, 1991).

Creating and maintaining a patchy habitat of grassland and scrub offers good cover and a diverse food supply for mammals. Where management leads to increased grass cover, field voles may reach high densities and exclude other species; while more scrub cover encourages woodmice, bank voles and field voles to coexist at high densities (Gurnell, 1985).

Common dormouse

The common dormouse (Plate 18) spends most of its life among the branches and foliage of shrubs and trees. Consequently, it is important to ensure an appropriate physical structure including sprawling bushes with plenty of lateral branches offering arboreal routeways for the animals to move about (Bright and Morris, 1989). Ride widening and management can therefore result in barriers to the movement of dormice (Mayle and Gurnell, 1991; Warren and Fuller, 1993). As a species with a localised and intermittent distribution (home range about 0.5 hectare; Morris, 1991), it is important to provide linkages between patches of suitable habitat, and rides should be managed to provide arboreal 'bridges' at intervals along their length. These may be provided by canopy trees, shrubs or even single branches (Warren and Fuller, 1993). A diversity of woody plant species should be encouraged, in order to provide a continuous sequence of flowers and fruits for dormice from April until November (Bright and Morris, 1989).

Bats

Woodland edges are important habitats for bats, both as roost sites and foraging areas (Plate 19). The provision of corridors of native broadleaved trees and shrubs such as birch, willows and wild cherries is especially valuable in providing habitats for moths, so increasing food availability for bats (Mayle and Gurnell, 1991). Riparian edges are particularly important for foraging bats, and clumps of broadleaved species around ponds and along streamsides in conifer plantations will further improve these areas. If well designed and managed, waterside and open scrub habitats provide sheltered foraging areas with an abundant supply of insect prey. Grassy areas which are mown regularly and receive sunlight may be good habitats for craneflies and ground beetles, both of which are important for foraging bats at certain times of the year (Mayle, 1990).

Deer

Edges and rides are attractive to deer, providing a food supply and cover. Deer have a fundamental influence on vegetation structure and composition at edges and in open areas, with low deer densities being generally beneficial and high deer densities being seriously detrimental (see Table 6.2). For this and silvicultural reasons some form of management programme is a necessity in most wooded areas. For further information see Practice Note 6: *Managing deer in the countryside* (Forestry Commission, 1999).

Reptiles and amphibians

Several reptile species use open areas along woodland edges, particularly on heathland sites, and high densities are associated with broad, sunny rides with wide, uncut verges of heath vegetation. Ride verges in conifer plantations in Dorset have been studied as habitats for common and sand lizards (Dent and Spellerberg, 1987, 1988). For the scarcer sand lizard, the ride verge characteristics of most relevance are the vegetation and soil types, the verge area and the number of sunshine hours received. In southern Britain, the sand lizard is strongly associated with a dry heathland type dominated by heather (Frazer, 1983). Consequently, the sand lizard has been found to show a clear preference for south-facing ride- and roadside banks where the vegetation is dominated by heather, bell heather, bilberry and bracken with areas of open ground (Plate 20; Dent and Spellerberg, 1987). The preference for the sunny aspect is to take maximum advantage of the warmth of the early morning sun. The same preference is shown, but to a lesser extent, by the common lizard, although this species tends to occur in areas where the edge vegetation is dominated by purple moor-grass, cross-leaved heath, dwarf gorse and various grasses (Dent and Spellerberg, 1987).

Similar broad habitat characteristics influence the use of edges by adders. In damp broadleaved woods, rides and roadside verges can be valuable refuges for grass snakes and piles of cut plant material can be left as egg-laying sites. Where ride or roadside ditches are permanently wet, they may provide suitable areas for common frogs (Warren and Fuller, 1993).

Animals in woodland edges and open areas: summary

- Vertical structure, horizontal patchiness and species composition of vegetation on forest edges are important in determining their value for wildlife.

- For vertebrates, the plant species present is often of secondary importance to vegetation structure in determining habitat value. Vegetation species composition is important for most phytophagous and nectar or pollen feeding invertebrates.

- Management for invertebrates needs to distinguish between the habitat needs of woodland and woodland edge species and those dependent upon open habitats such as grassland. Forests can contain important remnants of semi-natural grassland and heathland.

- Generalist species of invertebrates will often benefit from the provision of nectar from many early successional plant species.

- Many invertebrates have specific food plant requirements. Provision for specific species may require careful and subtle management intervention.

- Both edge width and structure are important for birds, with a shrubby margin being essential. Maintenance of a linear coppice belt, cut in alternate 10–20 m strips, may favour migrant songbirds.

- Ride and external edge management for general conservation objectives can also satisfy habitat requirements for pheasants. Rides should exceed 30 m in width to be beneficial, and pheasant density can be increased by maximising edge length and the extent of shrub cover within the edge zone.

- Although unlikely to affect mammal species richness, edge management will change their distribution and relative abundance, and may also influence the ease of predation.

- The management of forest rides needs to be modified where common dormice are found. An interconnecting tree canopy must be retained in places to provide arboreal 'bridges' for the animals to move about.

- Bats can utilise forest edges, both as roost sites and foraging areas. Edges fringed with native broadleaved trees and shrubs are valuable in providing habitats for moths, so increasing food availability for bats.

- Forest edges, particularly on heathland sites, can be attractive to several reptile species for basking areas. South-facing edges have been shown to be especially valuable.

- Networks of open space can have value as wildlife corridors, helping to reduce the negative effects of fragmentation of both heathland and grassland habitats.

Plate 1 *A shaded woodland ride, Straits Inclosure, Alice Holt Forest, Surrey/Hampshire.* (C.I.CARTER)

Plate 2 *Managed coppice: many plants and animals in British woodlands have become adapted to the regular disturbance and open ground conditions created by coppicing, conditions often absent from high-forest management.* (FOREST RESEARCH PHOTO LIBRARY 38175)

Plate 3 *A well-established ride in ancient semi-natural woodland, Wakerley Great Wood, Northampton-shire.* (R. FERRIS)

Plate 4 Wet, unplanted areas can provide valuable wildlife habitats within forests. Bentley Wood, Wiltshire. (C.I. CARTER)

Plate 5 Timber loading bays provide valuable temporary open space. Alice Holt Forest, Surrey/Hampshire. (C.I. CARTER)

Plate 6 Powerline corridors require management of regenerating scrub and can provide permanent networks of open ground within forests. Haldon Forest, Devon. (R. KHAN)

Plate 7 *Marsh fritillary*, Eurodryas aurinia. *This butterfly utilises damp unimproved meadows and boggy hollows, and is one of our most rapidly declining species. Suitable habitats may be found within some forests.* (C.I. CARTER)

Plate 8 *The pearl-bordered fritillary*, Boloria euphrosyne, *breeds in woodland clearings or unimproved grassland habitats with scattered scrub or abundant bracken. It is the subject of a species Action Plan as part of the UK Biodiversity Action Plan.*
(MARTIN WARREN/BUTTERFLY CONSERVATION)

Plate 9a *Black knapweed*, Centaurea nigra, *a valuable nectar source for butterflies, found in open grassland habitats with forests.*
(FOREST RESEARCH PHOTO LIBRARY 31319)

Plate 9b *Common dog-violet*, Viola riviniana, *is an important food plant for fritillary butterflies.*
(FOREST RESEARCH PHOTO LIBRARY 34037)

Plate 10 *A newly created forest ride cut into a pole-stage beech plantation, Black Wood, Micheldever, Hampshire. The ride system was created to meet a width equal to the height of the adjacent stand.* (C.I. CARTER)

Plate 11 *Vegetation succession in the same ride system, six years later, Black Wood, Micheldever, Hampshire.* (R. FERRIS)

Plate 12 *A fenced exclosure plot in a forest ride in Black Wood, Micheldever, Hampshire, showing the impact of browsing by deer and rabbits on woody regeneration along the forest edge. Photograph taken six years after the exclosure was established.* (R. FERRIS)

Plate 13 *A well-developed shrubby edge along the perimeter of a forest ride in Firestone Copse, Isle of Wight.* (C.I.CARTER)

Plate 14 *Open grassy habitat alongside a widened forest ride in Dodsley Wood, Hampshire. Such habitat is of value to a wide range of butterfly species that prefer open, sunny conditions.* (C.I. CARTER)

Plate 15 *Ringlet,* Aphantopus hyperantus, *a local but fairly common butterfly in much of England, Wales, Ireland and southern Scotland. They are found in woodland glades, rides and borders, where the ground vegetation is tall and lush (scrubby, rank grassland or hedgerows).* (S.H. CARTER)

Plate 16 *Ride or road intersections may be utilised to create large glades or box-junctions by cutting off the corners of adjacent compartments. Oakley Wood, Bernwood Forest, Oxfordshire.* (C.I. CARTER)

Plate 17 *A widened ride managed for pheasants*, Phasianus colchicus.
(THE GAME CONSERVANCY TRUST, FORDINGBRIDGE, HAMPSHIRE)

Plate 18 *Common dormouse*, Muscardinus avellanarius. *Arboreal 'bridges' of hazel*, Corylus avellana, *can help provide crossing points in rides.* (CHRIS PIERCE/SUSSEX WILDLIFE TRUST)

Plate 19 *The retention of large, old trees alongside forest edges and open areas is important for wildlife, where this does not conflict with safety considerations. Most woodland bats in Britain use large, old trees as roost sites.* (FOREST RESEARCH PHOTO LIBRARY 41511)

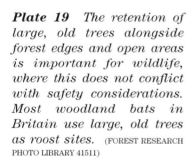

Plate 20 *Sand lizard*, Lacerta agilis. *Patches of bare ground along ridesides and roadsides on heathland sites provide valuable basking areas.* (A.W. JOLLANDS)

Plates 21, 22, 23 *Ride-widening operations at Bushey Leaze, Hampshire. Narrow, shaded rides may be enhanced by cutting back edge trees to create open conditions.*
(FOREST RESEARCH PHOTO LIBRARY 38936, 38947, 38962)

Plate 21

Plate 22

Plate 23

Plate 24 *Ride mowing using a tractor and swipe at Black Wood, Micheldever, Hampshire.* (FOREST RESEARCH PHOTO LIBRARY 39674)

Plate 25 *Cutting invasive scrub using a tractor-mounted long-reach flail cutter at Pembrey Forest, Dyfed.* (R. FERRIS)

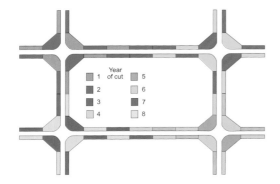

Plate 26 *A cyclic system for managing rideside vegetation: linear coppice strips and box-junctions cut on eight-year rotation (after Greatorex-Davies, 1991).*

Plate 27 *Forage harvesters may be used to cut and collect vegetation on sites where build-up of nutrients may pose a threat to floristic diversity.* (R. FERRIS)

Part Two

The Management of Edges

Chapter 6
Deciding on a management strategy

It is important to set clear objectives and specific goals at the outset of any management intended to bring conservation benefits. This will be influenced by judgements of what is feasible, ecologically appropriate, cost effective, affordable and compatible with other management objectives over the time scale required for the desired benefits to accrue. The process begins with an objective assessment of management potential, both ecological, organisational and financial, as outlined in Table 6.1.

Table 6.1 Establishing the potential for edge management.

Consideration	Good potential exists:
Conservation priority	• In and adjacent to ancient semi-natural and other native woodlands, which may act as a source of plant and animal species. • When scarce edge and open space species and communities are present. • When conservation is a high priority for the site owners or for the particular site. • When recreation and amenity are high priorities, since edge habitats are highly visible. • Where woodlands are adjacent to semi-natural open habitats, and the aim may be to develop a well-structured edge.
Landscape sensitivity	• Where landscape sensitivity due to public use or prominent location means the visual design of edges and open space will be a management priority.
Availability of resources and ability to make long-term commitment to management	• When resources are specifically targeted for edge management, i.e. where it has a high priority compared to other conservation measures. • When there is a long-term commitment to conservation management of this type, since edge management requires ongoing intervention and monitoring.
Expertise	• When in-house or local expertise is available for advice and monitoring.
Equipment	• For large enterprises that can justify purchase of edge management equipment. • For mixed enterprises with access to appropriate agricultural equipment. • In localities where there is a strong forestry and land management contracting sector.
Integration with other forest operations	• When edge and open space management does not conflict with access for and execution of other forest operations. • When other forest operations are likely to jeopardise edge and open space management objectives.

Table 6.2 Edge and open-space management priorities and opportunities.

Management aspect	1. Where potential biodiversity gain is low	2. Where biodiversity potential is high (in addition to 1)
Design of edges and open space *Chapter 7* *pages 42–43*	• Focus design effort on external edges adjacent to semi-natural habitats, or those receiving a high priority for visual appearance. • Focus design effort on inherent internal edges that are likely to be sustained with little or no management input. • Ensure that management to reduce wind throw risk also benefits wildlife. • Make the most of opportunities for providing edge habitats where management is required for other reasons, e.g. deer control glades, loading bays, turning areas, road junctions where visibility must be maintained, and under power lines (Luken *et al.*, 1991).	• Undertake proactive design of external, inherent and induced edges. • Accord external edges high priority when next to semi-natural or other woodland habitats. • In planted woodlands, build in plans for diverse edges at time of planting and thinning. • Retain wind-firm edges as permanent edge habitats. • Plan to provide areas of sunny sheltered conditions, bearing in mind requirements and location of high priority species or communities. • Create open space and edge habitat networks connecting open space features within the woodland and linking with any adjacent semi-natural open habitats.
Creating vegetation zones *Chapter 8* *pages 46–49*	• Where edges and rides (including intersections) have to be managed for operational reasons, manage on a two zone system to maintain herbaceous vegetation and promote a marginal scrub zone. • Promote spatial diversity by avoiding treating all managed edges during one year.	• Manage edges on a three zone system with short turf, intermediate tall herb and scrambler, and marginal scrub zones. • Promote wide ecotones. • Where the forest interior has little structural diversity, widen marginal scrub into two zones managed on 4–8 and 8–20 year rotations. • Manage each vegetation zone on a rotational basis, cutting 50–100 m strips.
Edge scrub zone management *Chapter 8* *pages 46–48*	• Ensure that operational scrub management (e.g. to maintain access, visibility and ingress into crops) is carried out to maximise structural diversity and promote species diversity. • Promote and protect areas of scrub vegetation where it does not compromise stand management, and where it is close to other habitats of high conservation value.	• Aim to achieve 50 % scrub cover along edges. • Cut between August and March to minimise impacts on fauna and allow seeding of flowering plants. • Avoid winter cutting on waterlogged sites. • Pile brash at the woodland edge, or chip and blow back into the tree stand. If burnt, keep number of fire sites to a minimum.
Managing grass and herb vegetation *Chapter 8* *pages 49–50*	• Ensure that operational ride and open space management, e.g. to maintain access, deer glades (Ratcliffe, 1985), riparian zones or ditches, is carried out in a way that promotes structural and species diversity of the herb layer.	• Establish annual or biannual mowing regimes to maintain short turf/tall herb communities. • Remove cuttings from site if they could compromise conservation aims by nutrient enrichment or smothering of sensitive species. This may be best achieved using a small forage harvester. • If not provided by forest operations, create small patches of bare ground to allow colonisation by desirable species. • Selective herbicides can be used for subtle manipulation of sward species composition in specific high priority areas.

Table 6.2 continued

Management aspect	1. Where potential biodiversity gain is low	2. Where biodiversity potential is high (in addition to 1)

Herbivore management
 	
Chapter 8 pages 53–55
	• If operational deer management strategies do not prevent excessive browsing of broadleaves, consider increasing culls. However, some level of browsing of scrub vegetation may be desirable, in order to maintain open conditions.
	• If increased culling is not possible consider fencing strategically important areas to promote scrub regeneration.
		• Introduce deer culling regimes that are low enough to achieve densities that will allow natural regeneration to occur.
		• Try to avoid exclusion of deer from large areas by fencing, as deer at low densities promote species and structural diversity. Temporary fencing of small areas may be required to allow natural regeneration in the short-term.
		• Consider using domestic herbivores if:
		  – you are sure that they will help achieve specific conservation goals;
		  – you have the organisational capability and expertise to manage livestock;
		  – you have confidence that livestock will not be detrimental to meeting other management objectives;
		  – you have the infrastructure to control stock movements.
		• Grazing species such as cattle, sheep and horses are usually less damaging to woody growth than browsers.
		• Running stock at low density over large areas for long time periods is probably the most practical option.
		• However, using stock at higher density in smaller enclosures at specific times of year can allow more refined vegetation manipulation.

Having evaluated the site potential for edge management, the design and management approach needs to be formulated. Necessary considerations are fully described in Chapters 7, 8, and 9. Table 6.2 provides an outline to guide the reader through Chapters 7 and 8.

Once the appropriate management prescriptions have been established, the manager must decide how and to what extent these should be applied on the ground. We recommend the following four-point course of action:

1. Identify areas where edge management is of highest priority.

2. Identify a basic network of existing open spaces linking these sites, or build this network with new open areas.

3. Consider whether desired prescriptions can be applied to this network given financial and logistical constraints, or whether opportunity exists for additional areas to be managed.

4. Make adjustments to ensure coherent management areas for efficient working.

Chapter 7
Design principles

The visual impact of edges

The management of edge habitats must be sensitive to their visual importance in the landscape both in defining afforested landscape units and as a focal point for forest users. Practical guidance is given in *Forest landscape design guidelines* (Forestry Authority, 1994), *Lowland landscape design guidelines* (Forestry Authority, 1992a), *Community woodland design guidelines* (Forestry Commission, 1991) and *Forest recreation guidelines* (Forestry Authority, 1992b) with the main elements to consider being shape, visual force, scale, diversity and unity. The design of external margins and internal open space should ensure that the forest fits well within the surrounding landscape (Forestry Authority, 1992a) and complements rather than conflicts with the local landscape character. Improvements to the landscape of edges, ecotones and open space are also likely to bring wildlife conservation benefits.

A distinction is drawn between margins which define the overall shape of a space, and edges which are made up of individual elements of single trees and small groups (Forestry Authority, 1992a). The design process must begin with the planning and formation of margins. Steep terrain makes the internal dimensions of forests more visible from outside the forest than on level ground. Under these circumstances greater attention should be given to the visual design of edges in relation to other features of the landscape beyond the forest.

External forest edges are usually visible, and design of the margin must be carefully planned and formed before details of edge treatment can be superimposed. Avoiding abrupt external edges

has wildlife as well as visual benefits. Well-structured edges, with a developed broadleaved tree and shrub zone, prevent adverse weather conditions (especially wind) from penetrating the forest, and provide a wide gradation of ecological niches. In order to diversify the actual edge and to build in long-term structural diversity, the aim should be to establish irregularly spaced and sized groups and individual trees (Figure 7.1).

The opportunity should not be missed to establish ecologically and visually diverse edges at the time of planting. This is particularly important where later thinning may increase the risk of windthrow. Where thinning operations are carried out, there may be opportunities to improve the landscape aesthetics and wildlife value of forest edges.

Using site and stand variation to enhance diversity

The predominant tree species, size of woodland, and silvicultural methods used will influence decisions about landscaping of edges, ecotones and open space. For example, thicket stage or under-thinned stands of dense, shade-casting species such as western hemlock (*Tsuga heterophylla*), Douglas fir (*Pseudotsuga menziesii*) and spruces (*Picea* spp.) may produce a very abrupt, narrow transition zone because they prevent the development of understorey vegetation. There may be limited visual variety along such edges, and the scope for improvements will be greater. In contrast, horizontal patchiness may naturally develop along the edges of less densely crowned species or where the tree crop has a varied vertical structure, so less intervention will be needed. In situations where natural woody growth occurs at forest edges either as remnants

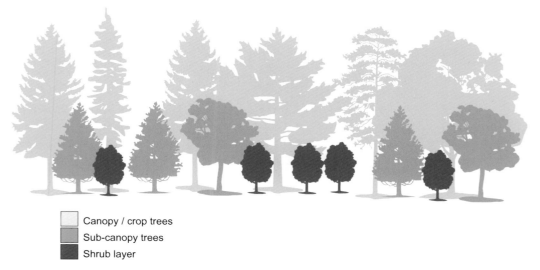

Canopy / crop trees
Sub-canopy trees
Shrub layer

Figure 7.1 View of an idealised external forest edge showing irregularly spaced and sized groups and individual trees and shrubs, providing visual and ecological diversity with a more stable longer-term structure.

of former semi-natural vegetation or regeneration, this can be managed to good effect in order to break up uniformity.

Edges on uneven, varied terrain present opportunities to vary both species and structural elements in response to variations in site and micro-climatic conditions. Capitalising on inherent site variation is likely to reduce the subsequent management input required to maintain edge diversity.

In areas where windthrow hazard is moderate to high, certain forms of edge management such as complete cutting back of edge trees may not be possible. To obtain wind-firm edges in stands at moderate to high risk:

- retain existing wind-firm edges where possible (e.g. those formed by roads, rides, watercourses and major changes in age or yield classes);

- use respacing and early thinning along edges to reduce edge density and increase edge tree stability;

- use shrub planting and gradual changes in planting density to create diffuse edges (Gardiner and Stacey, 1996; Quine and Gardiner, 1992). Opportunities should be made to include shrub species known to have particular benefit to wildlife.

Roads and rides

Managing rides and roadsides as wildlife corridors must be approached first at a landscape scale, recognising the importance of ensuring habitat connectivity with a network of linear linkages (Bennett, 1990; Dawson, 1994; Spellerberg and Gaywood, 1993; Verkaar, 1990), before specifying detailed management prescriptions. This requires that a hierarchical approach is taken, identifying those rides and roadsides which form the basic strategic framework, and overlaying these with secondary links which may be less intensively managed (either in time or space), and specific habitat areas which require management to meet particular objectives (e.g. conservation of a single plant species or community type).

Most forest rides have some degree of grass and herb cover, and are used infrequently for traffic. Because they are sheltered and sometimes sunlit, they have a good potential for supporting flowering plants and other wildlife. In order to maximise the value of this asset, make the most of variation in ride width, profile and direction. Of most potential value are rides that are gently curved, rather than characterised by sudden changes of orientation, especially if they link a succession of open spaces of different sizes. In many instances, variation in edge structure will

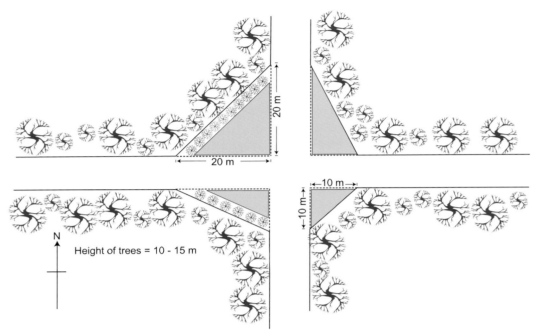

Figure 7.2 The creation of large corner glades or box-junctions at the intersections of forest rides or roads by the removal of edge trees. Visual diversity may be enhanced or improved by the creation of asymmetric glades rather than even-sized segments.

tend to occur even without management intervention, due to inherent site variability and the impact of disturbance agents (e.g. wind, mechanical damage and disease).

Amounts of sunlight reaching the ground can be increased by cutting bays or scallops in the ride edges, with solar radiation received being related to orientation (for explanation see Aspect, slope and latitude in Chapter 3 and Figure 3.2). Bays provide sheltered, sunny conditions, in which vegetation and dependent fauna can flourish, and should be irregularly spaced and varied in size. Opposing bays either side of a ride can produce large glades which receive more sunlight.

Major glades can be created at ride intersections (box-junctions) by removing the corners of the tree stands (Plate 16). Up to four separate segments can be managed together or in rotation (see Chapter 5). These not only add to the visual diversity, but also allow the sun to strike the ground from most angles. Asymmetric glades are preferable to even-sized segments on all corners

in order to add visual variety and a wider range of ecological conditions (Figure 7.2).

Subsequent ride management, as well as initial edge formation, can improve the wildlife potential and aesthetic quality. For example, a path of mown vegetation, usually grasses and small herbs, can be designed to pass irregularly from one side of the ride to the other, avoiding straight lines through the centre of the ride (which also increases total edge length). Groups of broadleaved trees and shrubs can be located and combined in an irregular, interlocking pattern. The aim throughout is to create a diverse edge, both in vertical structure and horizontal patchiness.

Forest edges along roadsides should provide a varied sequence of views, with a succession of varied spaces. This becomes especially important where a public road passes through the forest, in which case the edges should be planned on a broad scale (Forestry Authority, 1992b). Where it is important for rapid revegetation along the roadside edge, clumps of semi-natural vegetation can be regenerated from the topsoil removed from the roadline (see Forestry Practice Guide: *Forest roads*, Forestry Commission, in prep.). Localised scarification can reduce dominance of bracken and, through regeneration from buried seed, result in a temporarily diversified herb layer vegetation. Sometimes, tree and shrub planting may be desirable, in order to create a bolder effect, to tie the road in with features such as hedgerows and to encourage colonisation by woodland plant species. Roadside bays can be created in the same way as for rides, creating more varied edges. Where side views are being created through the forest, these should be funnel-shaped, widening further from the road, in order to make them readily visible to motorists (Forestry Authority, 1994).

The corridor between forest trees through which the forest road passes should be wide enough for the road to be open to the sun and wind to promote drying of the road surface (Forestry Commission, 1999). This may necessitate the cutting back of edge trees 10–30 m from the centre line of the road, particularly on roads with an east–west orientation, where the tree canopy on the southern side can keep the road under shade and lead to its rapid deterioration (Rowan, 1976). The greatest width is required for tall trees at northerly latitudes.

Design principles: recommendations

- Plan margin design and formation at a landscape scale, using opportunities to create networks of edge habitats, before formulating detailed edge management prescriptions.

- Be aware of the visual impact of edge design, particularly at forest margins.

- Think ahead: where possible build plans for diverse edges at the time of planting and thinning.

- When planning edge habitats, make the most of inherent variability in the site, and variability in current tree cover. This will reduce the management effort required to maintain diverse edge habitats.

- In windy areas, retain wind-firm edges where possible as permanent edge habitats. Management of edges to improve wind-firmness also usually increases their conservation value.

- In the strategic planning of edge and open space habitats make the most of variations in ride width, profile and direction.

- Keep in mind the importance to many species of sunny sheltered conditions. Management prescriptions should focus on situations where these conditions are available.

- Ride junctions provide good opportunities to develop edge habitats.

- Try to ensure that management prescriptions enhance rather than suppress structural diversity.

- On forest and public roads look for opportunities to bring wildlife benefits from plans and operations primarily for visual landscape or road maintenance purposes.

Chapter 8

Vegetation management

If the open, sunny conditions made by ride widening or gap creation are considered desirable (Plates 10–12 and 21–23), intervention is usually required to change or stop the vegetation succession towards scrub and woodland, particularly where browsing pressure is low. Cutting (coppicing) of woody vegetation and mowing of herbaceous vegetation is the main way in which succession can be altered, and this also helps to maintain diverse plant communities (Plates 24 and 25). However, the timing, sequencing and frequency of cutting can greatly affect vegetation development and conservation value. The regime chosen must be a compromise between sometimes conflicting ecological, practical and financial considerations.

Creating vegetation zones

Management regimes are best formulated in terms of prescriptions for different edge vegetation zones. A simple prescription for narrow rides or areas of lower conservation priority is the *two-zone system* (Figure 8.1). The central portion should be cut at intervals between 1 and 3 years to maintain herbaceous vegetation, with the marginal zone cut at longer intervals to allow scrub development.

A *three-zone system* (Figure 8.2) goes further in creating a *graded edge* and is most appropriate for wider rides, roads and open spaces, and for areas of high conservation priority. The three-zone system uses a 1–2 year cycle to maintain *short turf* in the central zone. The adjacent area of 5–10 m width is managed on a 2–4 year cycle to encourage the development of a *tall herb and scrambler zone*. The *marginal scrub zone* is cut at longer intervals. The scrub zone itself can be divided into two management areas, particularly where the tree stand is unfavourable for light-demanding species or those requiring structural variation; the first 2–8 m nearest to the roadside or ride could be cut every 4–8 years (when vegetation reaches 4 m in height), while the next 2–8 m nearest to the trees could be cut on a much longer rotation (8–20 years). Such a treatment benefits those animals requiring mature shrubs, and allows some of these plants to seed into the adjacent area. In a coniferous plantation lacking a wide scrub zone, it may be beneficial to remove several rows of trees and plant with appropriate coppice species, native to the site for the development of future linear scrub edge habitats.

Each vegetation zone should be managed on a rotational principle to avoid gross fluctuations in the area of each vegetation type and to maximise the diversity of the ecotone (Plate 26) (Ferris-Kaan, 1992; Porter, 1993; Warren and Fuller, 1993). Cutting of each zone should be in 50–100 m strips, alternating from side to side, in order to maintain some continuity of habitat for wildlife, and adding some visual variety and low level shelter.

Managing scrub vegetation

Unless there are overriding conservation objectives specific to one or a limited range of species (such as those for which a *Biodiversity Action Plan* exists, e.g. sand lizard, pearl-bordered fritillary) then the aim should be to provide as wide a range of scrub types (species, ages and hence structure) as possible. Most edge tree and shrub species are likely to be of value to wildlife, especially invertebrates. Where possible, native trees and shrubs should be retained at edges, particularly if they are locally scarce or represent a link with the former land use prior to afforestation.

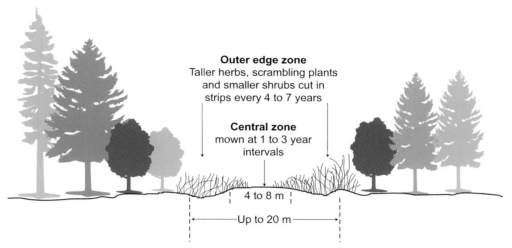

Outer edge zone
Taller herbs, scrambling plants and smaller shrubs cut in strips every 4 to 7 years

Central zone
mown at 1 to 3 year intervals

4 to 8 m

Up to 20 m

Figure 8.1 A simple two-zone cutting system, suitable for forest rides not managed specifically for wildlife. Modified from Warren and Fuller (1993).

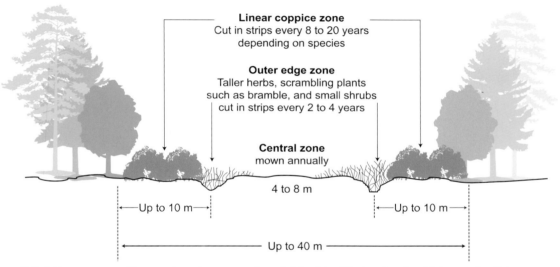

Linear coppice zone
Cut in strips every 8 to 20 years depending on species

Outer edge zone
Taller herbs, scrambling plants such as bramble, and small shrubs cut in strips every 2 to 4 years

Central zone
mown annually

4 to 8 m

Up to 10 m

Up to 10 m

Up to 40 m

Figure 8.2 A three-zone cutting system, for use on forest rides identified as having high or potential conservation value. Modified from Warren and Fuller (1993).

The cutting of scrub zones at woodland edges is best done between August and the end of March, to avoid disturbing nesting birds and to minimise impact on invertebrate populations. Scrub on heavy soils away from roads should be cut before waterlogging occurs. Diversity of shrub communities is best achieved by cutting segments of edge scrub each year, such that the whole is cut on an average duration appropriate to the growth rate and maximum size of material desired (Figure 8.3). In the case of riparian habitats, *Forests & water guidelines* (Forestry Commission, 2000) make the suggestion that stream channels should be approximately 50 % open, implying that adjacent scrub should be cut back to maintain such conditions. A similar rule of thumb might usefully be employed in forest rides and along roadsides, although in both cases there may be situations in which it is sensible to allow or promote native woodland to develop.

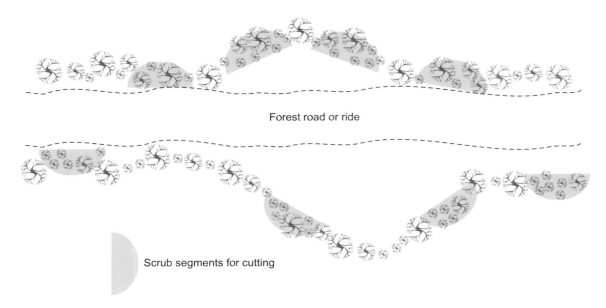

Forest road or ride

Scrub segments for cutting

Figure 8.3 Partial cutting of scrub vegetation to produce 'teeth' in order to create a more varied structure along a forest road or rideside edge.

Frequency of cutting operations may often be determined as much by the availability of suitable machinery (see Tools and techniques in Chapter 8) and labour as by the needs of nature conservation. This appeared to be the case in a series of Forestry Commission surveys of ride cutting operations (Currie, 1989; Ferris-Kaan and Warrener, 1990), in which a tendency to cut shrub zones at ride margins on a 3–5 year cycle was noted, the limit for much tractor mounted hedge-cutting and verge trimming equipment. This is ideal for certain plant and invertebrate species, as long as the logistics of machine use does not result in all edges being cut in the same year. However, it may be detrimental for some key plant species, e.g. violets that require the semi-shade from older coppice; and for some important bird species (Currie, 1991). For example, 6–8-year-old dense coppice growth is ideal for nightingales (Fuller and Warren, 1993), and probably also for warblers such as the blackcap and the garden warbler.

Dealing with brash

When cutting operations are necessary, the management of brash is an important consideration. Where rabbits are not a serious problem, brash may be piled, preferably right at the woodland edge where it will not damage field layer vegetation. Here it provides a semi-shaded deadwood habitat and additional side shelter to the woodland interior. Brash piled around coppice stumps provides only temporary and unreliable protection from browsing. Local markets may often be found for small dimension coppice material (Evans, 1984), particularly considering that the material is generally easily extracted to ride-side.

Where brash accumulation poses a serious problem, such as encouraging rabbits or bramble growth, then chipping may be considered, either for removal or blowing back into the stand (but see Chapter 9). A thin layer of bark chippings may have a particular value as a mulch (but should be avoided near to watercourses), controlling rank grasses and allowing more sensitive species to flourish. Certain plant species such as weld and wild mignonette have been observed to thrive under such conditions along forest ride and roadside edges (F.A. Currie, personal communication).

Burning of brash can increase soil pH by as much as three pH units immediately after burning, and bonfire sites can affect the soil to some depth. The major component of fresh white wood-ash is calcite, while potassium (K) and sodium (Na) carbonates are present in minor amounts. The initial very high pH values of wood-ash and surface soil are caused by K and Na oxides, hydroxides and carbonates which are very soluble and do not persist through periods of wet weather. Calcite is much less soluble and may be present three years after burning, maintaining moderately alkaline pH in surface soils that are normally neutral to strongly acid (Ulery *et al.*, 1993). Therefore, the burning of cut woody material is not recommended, especially on sites of conservation importance, where such action can lead to localised enrichment and the encouragement of rank vegetation. If burning is unavoidable, then it should be carefully controlled on a limited number of burn sites. These should be re-used when cutting operations are repeated. When scrub cutting along forest roads, the burning should take place on the road surface rather than the roadside verge.

Managing grass and herb vegetation

Mowing

Herbaceous vegetation must usually be periodically mown to prevent eventual succession to scrub and woodland (see Ecological principles in Chapter 4), although the frequency depends on whether the open space is to be maintained on a semi-permanent basis, or whether it is a temporary, possibly dynamic habitat (to be managed in various locations at different times). Where operational considerations such as access and fire-breaks predominate, the central 3–10 m of the ride may be mown annually (or biannually on heathland sites). However, where conservation is a priority more refined management is often beneficial (see Chapter 5). Numerous recommendations have been made (e.g. Steel and Khan, 1986; Carter and Anderson, 1987; Hall and Greatorex-Davies, 1989; Currie, 1991; Warren and Fuller, 1993), mostly based on the habitat requirements of invertebrates, particularly butterflies. These have often been adapted by woodland managers, in order to suit local

conditions, but little if any monitoring of the effects of mowing operations has been carried out.

Removal of cuttings is an important consideration on some sites (e.g. lowland heaths, chalkland, infertile clays), as plant species diversity is high due to low fertility suppressing aggressive species (Porter, 1993). Leaving cuttings promotes nutrient cycling and can increase fertility as well as smothering some smaller herbs, leading to dominance of a few competitive, rank species, with an associated depression of plant species diversity. Cut material should therefore be removed from sites where an increase in fertility would reduce species richness. This is less important on extremely impoverished species-poor sites such as upland heath, where an increase in nutrients can result in an increase in species richness. Nutrient input can be minimised by cutting and removal during the growing season, but this has to be considered against impacts on fauna.

Cutting in autumn and winter has least direct impact on woodland fauna (e.g. Warren and Fuller, 1993). However, as well as reduced nutrient off-take, compaction and associated damage to the ride or glade, roadside edge or riparian zone may occur as a result of the use of machinery over wet ground. Despite these factors, mowing operations have tended to be undertaken at this time, due to the availability of labour and machinery. The practice has been carried out in many forest sites in Hampshire and Sussex, resulting in rank growth of tufted hair-grass which is further favoured by roe deer browsing. Work in Bernwood Forest and Whitecross Green Wood, both in Oxfordshire, found that the best cutting regime for maintaining plant species diversity on these sites is a periodic July 'haycut' or cutting with a forage harvester, which favours early flowering broadleaved plants rather than grasses (Porter, 1993). The timing of summer cutting operations may be crucial, allowing spring flowering species to flower and set seed, but avoiding the summer flowering period of other species.

Decisions concerning timing and regularity of mowing operations need to be based on observational and survey evidence (see Chapter 9) of the value of the vegetation to wildlife. For example, a decline in numbers of a particular butterfly species might indicate that the abundance of its preferred foodplant has declined as a result of competition from dominant plant species in the sward. Actions would then be required to create conditions that favour the key plant species.

Only in very particular instances is the precise sward height important in determining habitat suitability for a species, e.g. turf height and amount of bare ground in relation to the abundance of violets as foodplants for the pearl-bordered fritillary (Greatorex-Davies *et al.*, 1992). This degree of precision may be difficult to achieve over large areas, if at all, and may only be appropriate to nature reserves and Sites of Special Scientific Interest (SSSIs). Generalised mowing regimes should normally be sufficient to meet the needs of a range of wildlife as long as they create diverse sward structures and promote diverse species composition.

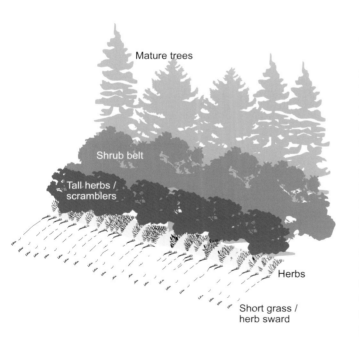

Figure 8.4 An idealised roadside edge, with parallel belts of different vegetation types to produce a graded edge structure.

Short turf and bare ground

Short turf with patches of bare ground provides a seedbed for new plants to colonise from buried seed or rhizomes, although if poorly managed it can encourage undesirable 'weed' species. Species such as wild strawberry require only small areas of bare ground in which to germinate and establish (Carter and Anderson, 1987). In a three-year study of the effects of various ride mowing treatments in Pembrey Forest, Dyfed, light scarification as a result of hand-raking of cut plant material led to an increase in abundance of devil's bit scabious, thought to be the result of the creation of suitable regeneration niches within the grass sward (Ferris-Kaan, 1992).

This short-turf zone should ideally be situated to receive maximum sunlight. For roadsides, the zone towards the top of the marginal ditch is best, extending back towards the trees for a distance of several metres and grading into zones of coarser vegetation (Figure 8.4). Where the site conditions enable machinery to be adequately manoeuvred, mowing operations should aim to vary the width and reduce the linearity of the vegetation zones. This avoids unnatural symmetry and allows different habitat patch sizes to develop, which may provide ideal conditions for a wider range of plant and animal species.

Mowing operations can be combined with some soil disturbance, to which many plant species are adapted. Species with buried seed reserves often require soil disturbance to trigger germination. Others, with underground tubers or rhizomes can be dispersed by soil disturbance and the breaking up of their underground parts. Alternatively, some problem species such as bracken, which often occurs along woodland edges, may be reduced in dominance and abundance by soil disturbance (Ferris, unpublished). Areas of bare mineral soil in sunny positions make good reptile basking areas (Dent and Spellerberg, 1987) and habitats for some invertebrates such as ground nesting bees (O'Toole and Raw, 1991).

In a field experiment on an ancient woodland site in Wakerley Great Wood, Northamptonshire, scarification of the roadside sward was carried out and the subsequent vegetation response monitored. This technique removed the vegetation cover and approximately 3–5 cm of topsoil in January, leaving bare ground. Within six months of the operation being carried out, almost complete vegetation cover had been achieved on most plots. Species richness was greater than for mown plots (Ferris, unpublished). A significant reduction in the cover of bracken had been achieved, and a number of species appeared in the sward, including pignut, a species regarded as a woodland relict in grassland sites (Grime *et al.*, 1988). Others increased in abundance, such as common dog-violet, which is able to regenerate through adventitious sprouting from the roots (Valentine, 1949), and was probably reduced in abundance in the denser, unmanaged parts of the sward in adjacent plots.

Soil disturbance may be achieved incidentally by forest operations, planned on a small scale using mowing equipment, or on a larger scale using scarification, cultivation or ripping implements. Complete removal of topsoil will rarely be practical but can create areas with depleted nutrient status favouring the development of a diverse groundflora. However, large areas of completely bare ground can allow colonisation by aggressive 'weed' species to the detriment of the more desirable grassland and woodland edge species. Carter and Anderson (1987) suggest creating scarified patches measuring 1–2 m², spaced at approximately 25 m intervals. Regular road maintenance in the form of regrading may have a particular value for scarce annuals and in some forest types such as those on sandy soils at Newborough (Anglesey), Pembrey (Dyfed), and Thetford (Norfolk). As with other operations, regrading a proportion of the road network at each visit is preferable to all roads being regraded in the same year.

Creating and managing zones: recommendations

- Manage narrow rides and roadsides of lower conservation priority on a two-zone system with herbaceous vegetation and marginal scrub zones.

- Manage wide rides and roadsides of higher conservation priority on a three-zone system with short turf, intermediate tall herb and scrambler, and marginal scrub zones.

- If the forest interior has little current or potential structural diversity, consider widening the marginal scrub zone into two zones managed on 4–8 and 8–20 year rotations.

- Manage each zone on a rotational basis based on cutting 50–100 m strips.

- Aim to provide as diverse a range of scrub habitats as possible, with about 50 % scrub cover along rides.

- Cut between August and March, avoiding winter cutting where ride damage will be severe.

- Pile brash at the woodland edge, except where ancient woodland plants are found.

- If brash piling is a problem, and it cannot be sold locally, then it can be chipped. Brash can be burnt but the number of fire sites should be minimised.

- Brash piles are not adequate protection for coppice regrowth against deer, and may encourage rabbits.

- Annual or biannual mowing is required to maintain herbaceous vegetation communities. Mow in July to promote plant species diversity, or from August if impacts on fauna are a serious concern.

- Cuttings can smother sensitive plants and increase nutrient cycling to the benefit of aggressive species, and should be removed in these situations.

- A tightly cut ground layer with some bare ground allows desirable species to colonise open space. On areas not disturbed by forest operations, create small patches of bare ground during mowing operations or use scarification equipment.

- Soil disturbance can reduce the dominance of aggressive species like bracken, but on a large scale can allow domination by a few 'weed' species.

Tools and techniques

Machinery for managing edge vegetation

A range of flail cutting machines has been used in the management of both scrub and grass/herb vegetation, and machine availability is often a primary determinant. Cutting of large diameter scrub requires robust and heavy machinery, which must be used in dry conditions to avoid serious compaction and rutting damage. When the scrub zone is separated from the ride or road by a ditch, a long-reach side-arm flail is required, or tractor access provided over the ditch. Machines are now available that extend up to 5–8 m from a tractor mounting (Plate 25). Most ride mowing operations are carried out using standard tractor-mounted swipe or flail cutters, with little or none of the material collected (Ferris-Kaan and Warrener, 1990). This machinery can operate on most surfaces likely to be encountered, apart from severe slopes. Tree stumps can be a problem on newly created rides for up to 10 years. During this period, the sward needs to be mown higher than would normally be the case, or more robust machinery used.

Removal of vegetation is often required on wildlife sites, particularly to prevent aggressive plant species from becoming too dominant. Agricultural forage harvesters have been evaluated for use in ride mowing operations, with a view to cutting and collecting the material in a single operation. They may be used to create a varied vegetation structure by selective driving and by adjustment of cutting height. They can be used 'in-line', i.e. immediately behind the mowing machinery, or 'off-line', where two tractors are used, the second pulling the harvester to one side of the mowing machinery.

These machines are generally not sufficiently manoeuvrable for restricted areas such as woodland rides, glades or roadsides, and they tend to be unstable on cambered surfaces such as ride and road edges. Furthermore, soft ground and often the small size of the site itself may preclude the use of standard machines. However, there are examples of smaller, lightweight forage harvesters

being successfully used for forest ride mowing operations (Plate 27). These can operate in restricted areas, may be linked to smaller and lighter tractors, and do not require the same degree of height clearance as agricultural machines. The type of cutting head used varies from reciprocating blade to vertical flails, with most machines having draught-assisted collection methods (Bacon, 1999). They are easy to operate, many having a straightforward tipping bin mechanism to dispose of the cuttings. One restriction is the relatively small capacity of the storage bin, which requires regular emptying. A trailer is needed if material is to be removed from the site.

A number of new machines are coming onto the market that are the equivalent of agricultural combine harvesters, with the capacity to work on large sites to cut and collect vegetation for removal off-site. They differ from previous machines in that they are not only specially designed for very-low-ground-pressure work on very wet and boggy sites, but they are also self-propelled and have PTO or hydraulic drives to enable the use of cutting, collecting and blowing attachments.

Woody cut material can be chipped. Small portable chippers, using the power take-off drive from a tractor or utility vehicle, are now readily available which can cope with material up to firewood size. Although most chippers are currently wheeled and need to be run onto wet sites using supports and platforms (Bacon, 1999), a tracked chipper is now available (the Arboreater 140). This is suitable for wet, boggy ground, enabling *in situ* chipping of brash and scrub. Wider tracks also reduce ground pressure and increase ground clearance to enable passage over stumps.

The creation of bare ground on wildlife sites may be desirable for a number of reasons, including the stimulation of dormant seeds in the soil seedbank and in the provision of habitat for warmth-loving invertebrates and reptiles. If ground disturbance is required during edge management operations, suitable lightweight scarifying machines are available. The Jacobsen scarifier has been used in field trials in Northamptonshire, where removal of bracken-dominated vegetation led to regeneration of a more species-rich roadside sward. Some of the smaller forage harvesters, such as the Amazone, also have the option of attaching scarifying blades in addition to the flails, which then give varying degrees of turf ripping during the same operation. Standard flail cutters, set deliberately low, can also produce a scarifying effect, particularly on uneven ground. While these techniques can completely remove the upper layers of vegetation and soil, alternatives now exist which reduce the volume of spoil and subsequent cost of disposal (Bacon, 1999). Rotoburying uses stone-burying machines to bury grass, turf and humus to a depth of 15-20cm, creating no spoil in the process. Turf-picking is another useful technique, involving the use of stone-picking machines to cut and lift turves, separating them from the soil and collecting them in a tipping hopper. This is a useful technique where nutrient burial is unacceptable. Turf-lifting can be used in the form of an attachment for a walk-behind power unit to cut grass and heath turves for manual rolling and lifting. While this is useful on uneven terrain and with coarse vegetation, it is likely to be time-consuming and hence only applicable on a small scale and on very special conservation sites.

For further information concerning machinery for conservation management see Supporting information, page 62.

Operational costs

The wide variation in site conditions across the UK mean that it is not possible to provide accurate costings. Instead, a range of current operational costs is given. The cost of mowing of grass rides is variable, depending upon terrain and precise objectives, but for general maintenance it is in the range of $25-75 per kilometre (km^{-1}). However, where mowing is to meet conservation objectives, e.g. on wide, botanically interesting, sometimes wet rides, periodic cutting can cost between $120 and $300 km^{-1}. Forage harvesting equipment may be as much as 70% more costly than conventional tractor-mounted swiping. The only figures available, (for managing chalk grassland rides and areas of lichen heath in East Anglia) estimate a cost of $35 km^{-1}. Scrub cutting along ride margins is a more costly operation, with costs ranging from $25 km^{-1} for tractor-mounted cutting up to $200 km^{-1} for motorised manual cutting using clearing saws or chainsaws. However, this figure can be even greater for scrub with semi-mature, overhanging woody growth, e.g. in the region of $500 km^{-1} in some cases. In many cases, clearance for ride widening or scalloping is achieved at no net cost by standing sale of material. A similar approach is often taken for riparian zone clearance, although costs have been estimated at between $175 and $250 km^{-1}.

These figures have been obtained from a survey of operational costs, provided by a sample of Forest Enterprise Districts in 1999.

Controlled grazing

In Chapter 5 the impact of different herbivore species on forest edges is described. Grazing produces subtly different effects to cutting, since many herbivores are selective. Under light or moderate grazing, floristic diversity is increased, with faster growing dominants removed, allowing slower growing but grazing tolerant species to compete. Apart from foliage removal, grazing animals have additional effects which may add to vegetation diversity, such as distribution of seeds and redistribution of nutrients through dunging, creating microsites for nutrient demanding plants (Bakker *et al.*, 1983).

Management of wild deer populations and impacts will usually be the most important part of the issue of grazing control. Even moderate deer numbers eliminate woody regeneration and hence jeopardise the development of structurally diverse edges. This is particularly acute at edges and open space as this is where deer spend much of their time feeding. The use of fences to control the impact of deer on edge and open space vegetation is rarely practical or cost effective, neither is total deer exclusion desirable as low densities of deer have a beneficial effect on ecotone structural and species diversity (Putman, 1996). Control of deer populations by culling is generally most effective, but this must be undertaken in the context of wider woodland management objectives, and often in collaboration with neighbours (Forestry Commission, 1999). In order to achieve a desirable density of deer (usually in the region of 2-4 red deer per 100 ha and 10-14 roe deer per 100 ha) current numbers must be estimated and cull levels set on this basis. Numbers and impacts must then be monitored and culling adjusted over time. This is known as *predictive deer management* and is described in Mayle (1996).

There are a number of examples of controlled use of domestic herbivores in vegetation management in woodland (e.g. Green and Newell, 1982; McCarthy, 1985; Adams, 1986; Bullock and Kinnear, 1988). Animals have been used on nature reserves, primarily to control vegetation succession and maintain species associated with early successional habitats, e.g. scrub control using goats in Tentsmuir National Nature Reserve, Fife (Bullock and Kinnear, 1988). Their use in woodland has sometimes been aimed at weed control, e.g. livestock grazing to aid plantation establishment (Doescher *et al.*, 1987), and more recently for re-creation, maintenance and enhancement of the characteristics of semi-natural woodlands.

Grazing animals could be used to achieve

Table 8.1 Examples of the use of herbivores for vegetation management (from Gill, 1991a).

Objective	Animal	Stocking density (number km^{-2})	Duration and season	Location	Reference
Birch/willow scrub removal in nature reserve	Goats	3200	3 months May-July	Fife, Scotland	Bullock and Kinnear (1988)
Firebreak maintenance	Goats	80–500	12 months	California, USA	Green and Newell (1982)
Weed control in young Douglas fir plantation	Sheep	13300	1 month	Oregon, USA	Sharrow *et al.* (1989)
Weed control in Sitka spruce plantation	Sheep	250–600	2-3 months	N. Ireland	Adams (1986)
Bracken control	Sheep	200–800	Until tree damage begins	New Zealand	Breach (1986)
Grass control	Cattle	1500	1 week	New Zealand	Dale and Todd (1986)
Gorse control		2000	–	New Zealand	Hansen (1986)
Grassland maintenance in nature reserves	Sheep Cattle	80–400 15–100	[a] [a]	UK	Massey (English Nature, personal communication)
Conversion of acid grassland to heathland	Cattle	100–200	12 months	Holland	Bokdam and Gleichman (1988)
Bramble control in forests	Goats	600	12 months	Victoria, Australia	McCarthy (1985)
Weed control in forests	Sheep	300–500	12 months	Western Australia	McKinnell (1975)

[a] Varies with grassland type.

vegetation management objectives at woodland edges and their associated habitats (Gill, 1991a; Table 8.1), but great care would need to be given to the selection of appropriate animals, stocking density, timing, duration of grazing, and the husbandry of the animals. For grazing of domestic stock to be an effective tool for vegetation management in woodlands it must be considered a high priority in terms of management input and resources. This will only rarely be the case in British conditions.

The grazing characteristics of different domestic herbivores are described in Chapter 5. Grazers generally do less damage to trees than browsers, as long as alternative palatable vegetation is always available. Primitive breeds are often able to utilise lower quality forage and are best adapted to withstand the sometimes harsh conditions (climate and poor food quality) in forests. Sheep will graze swards much shorter than cattle and are more selective, sometimes conspicuously avoiding plants like rushes. Horses can usually manage on poorer quality forage and are less selective, consuming many species like thistles, reeds and rushes that sheep and cattle avoid. They are also more hardy and can be left to graze year round in areas that would be unsuitable for cattle. Goats are primarily browsers and have been used successfully to control invasive scrub willow and birch in nature reserves. Both goats and horses are unfortunately more likely to strip bark than sheep or cattle. For further information see Technical Paper 25: *Grazing as a management tool in European forest ecosystems* (Humphrey *et al.*, 1998) and Information Note 28: *Domestic stock grazing to enhance woodland biodiversity* (Mayle, 1999).

Timing of deployment of domestic herbivores is important and related to local management objectives. For example, late summer or autumn grazing is usually recommended to allow for butterflies which require a grassland habitat. Conifer crops are most palatable just after bud-break and hence browsing should either be at this time to hinder growth of unwanted conifer regeneration, or should avoid this time to minimise damage to conifer crops.

Stocking rate is also an important consideration (Table 8.2), but to some extent depends on the productivity of the habitat and the favoured grazing regime. For example, an appropriate cattle stocking rate for a restricted period of grazing on unshaded ground would be in the region of 0.3–1.0 ha^{-1}. However, rates as low as 0.1 ha^{-1} or less would be suitable if animals are to be given free range over extensive areas.

Not all attempts at controlled use of herbivores have been successful. Problems have been reported with damage to trees, with reluctance to consume intended vegetation, and with the animals, including weight loss, abortion and even mortality. Whatever regime is adopted, regular monitoring is recommended to ensure that livestock are having the desired impact, and that livestock welfare is never compromised

A Forestry Commission study examined the impact of domestic goats on ride vegetation dominated by creeping willow in Pembrey Forest, Dyfed, an extensive sand dune system with particularly diverse ground vegetation. Tethered animals were grazed on rides for 4-5 weeks in April/May, and the resultant vegetation structure and composition was studied. Grazing reduced the vegetation height, with the partial removal of the creeping willow, but did not lead to significant increases in species diversity compared with plots which were mechanically mown. Some ground disturbance occurred, giving rise to some local variation in the vegetation. A number of problems were highlighted by this study, many of which have also been reported elsewhere. Not least of these is the need for careful monitoring of animal condition, to ensure that sufficient forage is available and that it is of a preferred type. Tethering the animals required considerable input on the part of the woodland manager.

Herbicides

Judicious use of herbicides and growth retardants may be a useful alternative to either cutting or grazing in the management of edge vegetation (Parr, 1988; Willis, 1991). With increasingly selective herbicides available, chemical control of undesirable vegetation should not automatically be considered ecologically unacceptable. For

Table 8.2 Summary of the broad categories of habitats found within forests and their general potential for domestic stock grazing management for nature conservation (from Young and Gordon, 1991).

Forest habitat feature	General physical features	Likely management differences between forest and agricultural situation	Potential for grazing management
Ride	Linear, becoming wider (but fewer in number) with restructuring management (20–30 m).	Not burned. Not grazed by domestic stock. Shaded by tree crop on either side. May receive fertiliser from aerial application to tree crops.	Vegetation communities which have become dominated by tussock grasses or woody shrub/scrub thickets would respond well to domestic stock grazing management where establishment and maintenance of a more open and varied vegetation structure and/or species composition is desired. There is also scope for appropriate stocking regimes to be used to manipulate the vegetation structure and composition to optimal levels for desired vertebrate and invertebrate groups or species. Young trees with leading shoots at or below domestic stock browsing level are likely to be at risk from damage by free-ranging stock. Young crops (with the canopy still open) on vulnerable soils may be at risk from root trampling damage, particularly at high stocking rates. If compartments with young crops can be fenced until past the vulnerable stage, domestic stock can be allowed to roam freely in the forest. This is likely to be less costly than fencing individual rides. Mechanical cutting of vegetation (to encourage more palatable and nutritious new growth) and supplementary feed can be used to attract animals to particular areas.
Roadside	Linear, mean overall width 9 m, verges are becoming wider during restructuring.	Ground disturbed during road building. Stone imported to the site to build the road. Shaded by tree crop. Drained along roadside. Not burned. Not grazed by domestic stock.	Very good potential for domestic stock grazing management due to road use and high fencing cost for linear features. Free-range stocking may be the most viable economic option and may have the added advantage of precluding the need for annual cutting of roadside vegetation, for the maintenance as firebreaks.
Wayleaves	Linear, generally wider than rides or roadsides, often one tree-height either side of the service.	Similar to rides but because they are wider less shading effect and thus greater scope for improvement of nature conservation value.	Reasonable potential for stock grazing management. Fencing may be a more feasible option for stock control with a larger grazable area per length of fence compared with rides or roadsides.
Stream-sides	Linear, narrow, planting now being kept back at least 20 m from the edge of major watercourses. Generally on better soil than other linear features.	As for rides but with greater widening during restructuring and thus less shading effect from the surrounding crop.	Good potential for diversification of vegetation structure and species composition of forest streamsides, dominated by grass tussock and/or scrubby vegetation, using domestic stock grazing. This is due to the generally richer soil conditions, the occurrence of both streamside and forest edge environments, the reduced shading effect of the adjacent tree crop and the generally high priority accorded to conservation in these areas.

example, studies in grass/rush dominated swards showed that gaps created by selective herbicides became rapidly invaded by a variety of flowering herbaceous species including primrose and violets (Ferris-Kaan *et al.*, 1991). Other advantages of chemical control include relative ease of operation in small and/or inaccessible areas, and the one-off nature of the operation in many cases.

Herbicides can be used to create bare areas as regeneration patches or bare ground habitats. If so, area of treatment is important, as demonstrated by studies in which the broad spectrum herbicide glyphosate was applied to edge and woodland plant communities, and resulted in domination by ruderals such as heath groundsel (Watt *et al.*, 1988).

However, it will seldom be necessary to eradicate vegetation cover for conservation purposes, and only a small range of species present a problem on woodland edges, e.g. grasses such as tufted hair-grass, purple small-reed and *Holcus* spp. or tall herbs and scramblers such as bracken and bramble (Watt *et al.*, 1988). Therefore, it will be more usual to use selective herbicides to achieve a more subtle manipulation of the vegetation. Recommendations are provided in Field Book 8: *The use of herbicides in the forest* (Willoughby and Dewar, 1995). Where a species cannot be selectively controlled, such as bramble, it may be possible to use spot application of a broad spectrum herbicide to achieve the same end.

Growth retardants may be used to reduce vegetation growth. Mefluidide has less effect on broadleaved species than other retardants (Marshall, 1983) and tends to give rise to a thinned sward with bare patches, allowing plants from dormant or incoming seed to germinate and establish (Parr, 1988). Its use has been suggested as a partial replacement to cutting, which would allow longer periods for flowering and seeding, and increased vigour of sub-dominant plants. However, it has also been noted that growth retardants may affect flowering of some species (Feldwick, 1988; Ferris-Kaan, 1991), and monitoring may be required where particular herbs are desired, for example as specific foodplants for invertebrates.

Tools and techniques: recommendations

- Flail cutters are most commonly used for edge management. Ensure equipment is robust enough to cope with scrub and stumps.

- If off-take is important to achieve conservation objectives consider whether a forage harvester can be used.

- Grazing is selective and has a different impact to mowing. Each herbivore species creates different selective pressures.

- For most habitat types a low level of grazing or periodic grazing is better than permanent and intense grazing or no grazing at all.

- Deer impact is a problem in most areas and must be managed if edge management is to be successful.

- Exclusion of deer by fencing is expensive and does not achieve optimal grazing levels. Deer population management by culling is usually required.

- Domestic herbivores can be used in woodlands but must be accorded a high management priority to avoid unacceptable impacts and ensure good animal husbandry.

- Selective herbicides are most useful for management of edges and open space. Herbicides are available that favour: herbs over grasses, fine grasses over coarse grasses, woody species over non-woody species, and that control problem species such as bracken.

- Growth retardants may be worth considering as a means of promoting sward diversity and reducing mowing frequency.

Chapter 9

Monitoring changes in plant and animal communities

Monitoring should be considered an integral and operational part of the management process. It can provide useful insights into the effects of management. For any type of monitoring, objective sampling systems are needed to yield reliable data for making comparisons over space and time. If specific plots are to be reassessed in the future they must be marked with an appropriate degree of permanence, e.g. FENO markers, steel rods with locking spikes to provide anchorage (see Supporting information, page 62). A vital part of designing any monitoring system is to plan for data storage and management, particularly where a commitment to long-term monitoring is being made.

Vegetation monitoring

Details of how to record the relative abundance and frequency of vegetation and advice on sampling edge vegetation are provided in Forestry Commission Bulletin 108: *Monitoring vegetation changes in conservation management of forests* (Ferris-Kaan and Patterson, 1992). These are the main attributes of vegetation that will be useful in monitoring:

- Abundance, distribution and performance of individual species, selected for specific reasons, e.g. indicators of ecological status, importance to certain animal species, rarity.

- Plant community features such as species richness, diversity and community composition. These parameters are derived from information on distribution and/or abundance of individual species.

- Vegetation structure; vertical layering (stand structure) and horizontal patchiness (woodland structure). Such features are important to animals and may often be used as a measure of habitat quality which is simpler and less costly to monitor than the animal populations themselves.

Monitoring of vegetation changes on forest edges, or any linear habitats (e.g. riparian zones, compartment boundaries) should take account of the different vegetation zones across the edge, as well as changes in species abundance. There are two main methods: firstly, for relatively stable edge zones which may be defined by deliberate management and, secondly, for mobile boundaries. In the first situation, sample areas may be divided into a number of quadrats, each replicated and matched with an adjacent untreated control sample area. In the second, where boundaries are unclear, or their movement over time is to be monitored, the layout consists of quadrats arranged end-to-end in parallel replicated 'ladder transects', perpendicular to the edge. Systematic sampling along such transects is useful to record the abundance of any species in relation to environmental gradients or topographical features. In situations where a limited number of clearly visible plant groups are to be monitored, line transects may be used.

Monitoring the responses of invertebrates to ride management

Targeted monitoring of invertebrate responses to ride management requires clarity of management objectives since only a small fraction of invertebrate species can be monitored. If these aims are broadly based, i.e. they have the intention of increasing the general variety of insect life present, little more than a few midday visits on warm sunny summer days with an experienced entomologist, before and two or three years after the changes are made, will produce valuable comparisons. Large, attractive, active insects that fly during warm summer days will be most noticed by visitors. In Britain, these will be Lepidoptera (butterflies and moths) and possibly Odonata (dragonflies and damselflies). In fact, the presence of a high number of butterfly species is generally regarded as indicative of a habitat with a rich wildlife. If management is specifically planned to create suitable conditions for a single species that merits special treatment on account of its rarity or in having some local significance, specific monitoring is needed. Between these extremes are various (now standard) techniques used by both amateur and professional entomologists, which are aimed at recording the diversity and abundance of particular invertebrate groups.

Butterflies and moths

A standardised sampling method for counting the numbers and species of adult butterflies along a set route throughout the year has been widely used for 18 years, and data from almost 100 sites located throughout the country comprise The Butterfly Monitoring Scheme (BMS) (Pollard, 1977). This depends upon a trained observer being available every week to choose a suitable midday period to walk, count and identify all the butterflies within a predetermined route. Year to year changes in response to forest or ride management need to be viewed with regard to regional trends as there is a pronounced synchrony of butterfly populations over large areas of Britain (Pollard and Yates, 1993). Certain species have notable fluctuations in numbers over the years; an extreme example of this is the holly blue, but other less obvious cyclic population trends probably exist. For full details of the methodology, see Pollard *et al.* (1986).

Night flying moths have also been sampled continually at a number of locations using the Rothamsted Light Trap (Williams, 1948) which incorporates a 200 W tungsten 240 V lamp with clear glass. The moths attracted to the lamp fly into a funnel and down into a darkened jar, where they are anaesthetised. Identification of these

catches from a network of traps on a daily basis has enabled regional patterns and population changes to be monitored.

Much larger nightly samples can be obtained using an ultraviolet light from mercury vapour lamps. A trap described in Robinson (1952) is much used for gathering information from selected sites. A smaller, battery powered, ultraviolet light trap with a small fluorescent tube, which can be taken to more inaccessible habitats, is described in Heath (1965).

Different lamps attract different species according to their brilliance and wavelength. With some species, only one sex comes to light and some species do not come to light at all. The number of moths collected in any one night is very much determined by the weather; overcast, calm, humid nights are the most favourable, whereas cool, clear, breezy nights, even if following a warm sunny day, are frequently unfavourable.

Other groups and sampling methods

Pitfall traps can be used to monitor ground dwelling insects and spiders (Southwood, 1978). Being static and unobtrusive, they can be left for between one and two weeks before the samples are taken away and the trap replenished. A more intensive monitoring technique uses sweeping nets or beating trays to dislodge insects from selected vegetation types (Southwood, 1978). Although these methods can be used to get relative estimates of numbers of insects, they are most useful for obtaining site faunistic lists. Much larger samples can be collected from ground vegetation using a circular vacuum sampler powered by a portable motor that is carried on a rucksack frame (Dietrick, 1961). Provided the vegetation is not wet, this method is good for sampling small arthropods.

Single species studies usually require skilled and specialised searching or sampling techniques in order to locate and count the number of individuals present in a unit of time, vegetation or area. This may sometimes mean some form of destructive sampling where vegetation is removed, or perhaps turf or litter is taken away for sorting or subjected to liquid or heat extraction methods. Perhaps the least damaging method in making comparative population estimates over short periods of time is the mark-recapture technique (Lewis and Taylor, 1967; Southwood, 1978).

Assessment of bird populations

Monitoring of bird populations can be set up in conjunction with local ornithological groups. Because birds respond most to changes in vegetation structure rather than plant species composition, recording structural changes in vegetation is of relevance. *Foliage height diversity* is an important parameter in this respect (Petty and Avery, 1990).

Point counts and *line transects* are the most appropriate methods of monitoring bird numbers. Point counts are suitable for use throughout the year, and they involve counting birds from fixed points on the ground during a specified time interval (Baillie, 1991). The duration of the counts is an important consideration: if the period is too short, individuals are likely to be missed, while if it is too long, densities are likely to be overestimated as individuals can be counted twice. Five minutes is considered adequate for most purposes (Fuller and Langslow, 1984).

Line transects involve observers walking a fixed straight line route and recording the birds that they see on either side of the line. Again, they can be used at any time of the year. They are best suited to large areas of continuous habitat through which observers can move without difficulty (Baillie, 1991). Three transect methods exist. Strip transects simply count all birds within a set distance from the centre line; birds seen outside the strip are not recorded. In fixed-distance line transects birds are recorded as being either within a central zone (usually 25m either side of the line) or beyond it. Variable-distance line transects involve recording either the perpendicular distance from each bird to the transect line, or categorising individuals into distance zones (Emlen, 1977).

Further details of methods for estimating bird numbers and measuring habitat features of critical importance to them can be found in: Dawson's (1985) review in *Bird census and atlas studies*, *Bird census techniques* by Bibby *et al.* (1992), and Forestry Commission Occasional Paper 26: *Forest bird communities* (Petty and Avery, 1990).

Small mammals

A number of well-developed methods exist for monitoring small mammal populations based on live capture and mark-recapture techniques (Southern, 1964; Montgomery, 1987; Gurnell and Flowerdew, 1994). Most of these methods require monitoring over five or more years to overcome the masking effect that population cyclicity will have on the relationship between habitat management and small mammal communities. Methods of recording movement have been reviewed by Wolton and Flowerdew (1985), the most widely used being to record the successive locations where a marked animal is live-trapped. There are limitations to this approach, not least that individuals can only be recorded where there are traps and the presence of bait is likely to disrupt normal behaviour patterns. Habitat preferences and population densities, as indicated by usage, can be calculated from assessments of the quantity and persistence of faecal pellet groups (Ratcliffe, 1987).

It is not uncommon for sudden switches in the relative abundance of yellow-necked mice *(Apodemus flavicollis)*, and wood mice *(A. sylvaticus)*, and wood mice and bank voles *(Clethrionomys glareolus)*, to occur in response to changes in the habitat (Gurnell, 1985). Field voles *(Microtus agrestis)* favour grassy vegetation and usually exclude other species as they increase in abundance (Hansson, 1977). These characteristic changes in community composition provide useful indicators of the effect of changes in the vegetation structure and plant species composition which may occur as a result of successional processes and/or management on woodland edges.

Monitoring changes in plant and animal communities: summary

- Monitoring the success of vegetation management operations on forest edges is essential to ensure that objectives are being met, and represents an integral part of the management process.

- Invertebrates, songbirds and small mammals can all be monitored using recognised, standard and repeatable methods. In all of these cases, expertise can be found among a number of local organisations, e.g. local wildlife groups or natural history societies.

- Care should be taken to ensure that records are kept in an easily retrievable form, preferably using a computer database.

- Monitoring can assist in the management process, by highlighting beneficial and undesirable changes in edge habitats, allowing necessary adjustments in management to be made, and allowing techniques thus proven to be successful to be used elsewhere.

Supporting information

Machinery for conservation management

Contact the Forum for the Application of Conservation Techniques (FACT), c/o John Bacon, FACT co-ordinator, English Nature, Northminster House, Peterborough PE1 1UA. Tel/Fax 01694-723101.

Permanent plot marking systems

FENO markers are available from:
Holtwood Marketing Ltd
11 Brassey Drive
Aylesford
Kent ME20 7QL
Tel: 01622 710921
Fax: 01622 717945

Useful addresses

Forest Research
Alice Holt Lodge
Wrecclesham
Farnham
Surrey GU10 4LH
Tel: 01420 22255
Fax: 01420 23653
www.forestry.gov.uk

Butterfly Conservation
UK Conservation Office
PO Box 444
Wareham
Dorset BH20 5YA
Tel: 01929 400209
Fax: 01929 400210
ukconsoffice@butterfly-conservation.org

The Royal Society for the Protection of Birds (RSPB)
The Lodge
Sandy
Bedfordshire SG19 2DL
Tel: 01767 680551
Fax: 01767 692365
www.rspb.org.uk

The Mammal Society
15 Cloisters House
8 Battersea Park Road
London SW8 4BG
Tel: 020 7498 4358
Fax: 020 7622 8722
www.mammal.org.uk

English Nature
Northminster House
Peterborough
PE1 1UA
Tel: 01733 455000
Fax: 01733 568834
www.english-nature.org.uk

Department of the Environment, Transport and the Regions (DETR)
Biodiversity Secretariat
Room 902D, Tollgate House
Houlton Street
Bristol BS2 9DJ
Tel: 0117 9876293
Fax: 0117 9878182
www.detr.gov.uk

The British Trust for Ornithology (BTO)
The National Centre for Ornithology
The Nunnery
Thetford
Norfolk IP24 2PU
Tel: 01842 750050
Fax: 01842 750030

Countryside Council for Wales
Plas Penrhos
Fford Penrhos
Bangor
Gwynedd LL57 2LQ
Tel: 01248 385500
Fax: 01248 355782
www.ccw.gov.uk

Scottish Natural Heritage
12 Hope Terrace
Edinburgh EH9 2AS
Tel: 0131 447 4784
Fax: 0131 446 2279
www.snh.org.uk

Environment and Heritage Service (Northern Ireland)
Commonwealth House
35 Castle Street
Belfast BT1 1GU
Tel: 01232 251477
Fax: 01232 546660
www.nics.gov.uk/ehs

REFERENCES

ADAMS, S.N. (1986). Sheep performance and tree growth on a grazed Sitka spruce plantation. *Scottish Forestry* **40**(4), 259–263.

ANDERSON, M.A. (1979). The development of plant habitats under exotic forest crops. In: *Ecology and design in amenity land management*, ed. S.E. Wright and G.P. Buckley. Wye College, Kent, 87–108.

ANDERSON, M.A. and BUCKLEY, G.P. (1991). Managing edge vegetation. In: *Edge management in woodlands*, ed. R. Ferris-Kaan. Forestry Commission Occasional Paper 28. Forestry Commission, Edinburgh, 5–10.

ANDERSON, M.A. and CARTER, C.I. (1987). Shaping ride sides to benefit wild plants and butterflies. In: *Wildlife management in forests*, ed. D.C. Jardine. Institute of Chartered Foresters, Edinburgh, 66–80.

ANGELSTAM, P. (1992). Conservation of communities - the importance of edges, surroundings and landscape mosaic structure. In: *Ecological principles of nature conservation – applications in temperate and boreal environments*, ed. L. Hansson. Elsevier, London, 9–70.

BACON, J. (1999). *Practical solutions handbook: equipment, techniques and ideas for wildlife management.* Forum for the Application of Conservation Techniques. English Nature, Peterborough.

BAILLIE, S.R. (1991). Monitoring terrestrial breeding bird populations. In: *Monitoring for conservation and ecology*, ed. F.B. Goldsmith. Chapman and Hall, London, 112–132.

BAKKER, J.P., DE BIE, S., DALLINGA, J.H., TJADEN, P. and DE VRIES, Y. (1983). Sheep grazing as a management tool for heathland conservation and regeneration in the Netherlands. *Journal of Applied Ecology* **20**, 541–560.

BEATTY, S.W. (1984). Influence of microtopography and canopy species on spatial patterns of forest understorey plants. *Ecology* **65**, 1406–1419.

BENNETT, A.F. (1990). *Habitat corridors: their role in wildlife management and conservation.* Department of Conservation and Environment, Melbourne, Australia.

BIBBY, C.J., BURGESS, N.D. and HILL, D.A. (1992). *Bird census techniques.* Academic Press, London.

BOKDAM, J. and GLEICHMAN, J.M. (1988). The effect of cattle grazing on the development of *Calluna vulgaris* and *Deschampsia flexuosa.* The Third European Heathland Workshop, August 1988, Denmark.

BREACH, T. (1986). Bracken fern control with livestock: Te Wara forest. *Proceedings Agroforestry Symposium*, 24–27 November 1986. *FRI Bulletin* **139**, 76–84.

BRIGHT, P. and MORRIS, P. (1989). *A practical guide to dormouse conservation.* Mammal Society Occasional Publication No.11. Mammal Society, London.

BROWN, A.H.F. and OOSTERHUIS, L. (1981). The role of buried seed in coppice woods. *Biological Conservation* **21**, 19–38.

BRYANT, J.P., CHAPIN, F.S. and KLEIN, D.R. (1983). Carbon/nutrient balance of boreal plants in relation to vertebrate herbivory. *Oikos* **40**, 357–368.

BUCKLEY, G.P. (1994). The effects of edge-management practices on the vegetation of lowland plantations and woods. Internal Contract Report to The Forestry Authority (Research Division), Project Y29/P4.

BUCKLEY, G.P., HOWELL, R., WATT, T.A., FERRIS-KAAN, R. and ANDERSON, M.A. (1997a). Vegetation succession following ride edge management in lowland plantations and woods. 1: The influence of site factors and management practices. *Biological Conservation* **82**, 289–304.

BUCKLEY, G.P., HOWELL, R. and ANDERSON, M.A. (1997b). Vegetation succession following ride edge management in lowland plantations and woods. 2: The seed bank resource. *Biological Conservation* **82**, 305–316.

BULLOCK, D.J. and KINNEAR, P.K. (1988). The use of goats to control scrub in Tentsmuir Point National Nature Reserve, Fife: a pilot study. *Transactions of the Botanical Society of Edinburgh* **45**, 131–139.

CADENASSO, M.L., TRAYNOR, M.M. and PICKETT, S.T.A. (1997). Functional location of forest edges: gradients of multiple physical factors. *Canadian Journal of Forest Research* **27**, 774–782.

CARTER, C.I. (1991). Ride orientation and invertebrate activity. In: *Edge management in woodlands*, ed. R. Ferris-Kaan. Forestry Commission Occasional Paper 28. Forestry Commission, Edinburgh, 17–21.

CARTER, C.I. and ANDERSON, M.A. (1987). *Enhancement of lowland forest ridesides and roadsides to benefit wild plants and butterflies.* Research Information Note 126. Forestry Commission, Farnham.

di CASTRI, F., HANSEN, A.J. and HOLLAND, M.M., eds (1988). A new look at ecotones: emerging international projects on landscape boundaries. *Biology International, Special Issue* **17**, 1–163.

CHEN, J., FRANKLIN, J.F. and SPIES, T.A. (1993). Contrasting microclimates among clearcut, edge, and interior of old-growth Douglas-fir forest. *Agricultural and Forest Meteorology* **63**, 219–237.

CHINERY, M. (1986). *Collins guide to the insects of Britain and Western Europe.* Collins, London.

CLEMENTS, D.K. and TOFTS, R.J. (1992). Hedges make the grade – a look at the wildlife value of hedges. *British Wildlife* **4**(2), 87–95.

COOPER, M.R. and JOHNSON, A.W. (1984). *Poisonous plants in Britain and their effects on animals and man.* Ministry of Agriculture, Fisheries and Food Reference Book 161. HMSO, London.

CURRIE, F.A. (1989). A survey of ride management practice in East England. Unpublished Forestry Commission Report. Forestry Commission, Cambridge.

CURRIE, F.A. (1991). Some economic factors in the long-term maintenance of edges. In: *Edge management in woodlands*, ed. R. Ferris-Kaan. Forestry Commission Occasional Paper 28. Forestry Commission, Edinburgh, 64–65.

DALE, R.W. and TODD, A.C. (1986). Using cattle to control pampas grass in Maramarua and Waiuku forests. *Proceedings Agroforestry Symposium,* 24–27 November 1986. *FRI Bulletin* **139**, 95–103.

DAWSON, D.G. (1985). A review of methods for estimating bird numbers. In: *Bird census and atlas studies*, ed. K. Taylor, R.J. Fuller and P.C. Lack. British Trust for Ornithology, Tring, 27–33.

DAWSON, D.G. (1994). *Are habitat corridors conduits for animals and plants in a fragmented landscape?* A review of the scientific evidence. English Nature Research Report 94. English Nature, Peterborough.

DENT, S. and SPELLERBERG, I.F. (1987). Habitats of the lizards *Lacerta agilis* and *Lacerta vivipara* on forest ride verges in Britain. *Biological Conservation* **42**, 273–286.

DENT, S. and SPELLERBERG, I.F. (1988). Use of forest ride verges in southern England for the conservation of the sand lizard *Lacerta agilis* L. *Biological Conservation* **45**, 267–277.

DIETRICK, E.V. (1961). An improved backpack motor fan for suction sampling of insect populations. *Journal of Economic Entomology* **54**, 394–395.

DOESCHER, P.S., TEASCH, S.D. and ALEJANDRO-CASTRO, M. (1987). Livestock grazing: a silvicultural tool for plantation establishment. *Journal of Forestry* **40**, 290–37.

EMLEN, J.T. (1977). Estimating breeding season bird densities from transect counts. *Auk* **88**, 323–342.

EVANS, J. (1984). *Silviculture and broadleaved woodland.* Forestry Commission Bulletin 62. HMSO, London.

EVANS, M.N. and BARKHAM, J.P. (1992). Coppicing and natural disturbance in temperate woodlands – a review. In: *Ecology and management of coppice woodlands*, ed. G.P. Buckley. Chapman and Hall, London, 179–198.

FELDWICK, G.A. (1988). Advantages and disadvantages of using the growth retardant mefluidide in areas of conservation interest. *Aspects of Applied Biology* **16**, 131–138.

FERRIS-KAAN, R., ed. (1991). *Edge management in woodlands.* Forestry Commission Occasional Paper 28. Forestry Commission, Edinburgh.

FERRIS-KAAN, R. (1992). The composition of ride vegetation: effects of different management regimes – Pembrey Forest, South Wales. Unpublished Research Report. Forestry Authority (Research Division), Farnham.

FERRIS-KAAN, R. and PATTERSON, G.S. (1992). *Monitoring vegetation changes in conservation management of forests.* Forestry Commission Bulletin 108. HMSO, London.

FERRIS-KAAN, R., PEACE. A.J. and NOWAKOWSKI, M. (1991). The use of herbicides to manage ride vegetation: preliminary results from Black Wood, Micheldever Forest. Unpublished Research report. Forestry Authority (Research Division), Farnham.

FERRIS-KAAN, R. and WARRENER, S.J. (1990). A survey of ride management practices by Forest Districts in England and Wales, 1989/90. Unpublished Research Report. Forestry Authority (Research Division), Farnham.

FORESTRY AUTHORITY (1992a). *Lowland landscape design guidelines.* HMSO, London.

FORESTRY AUTHORITY (1992b). *Forest recreation guidelines.* HMSO, London.

FORESTRY AUTHORITY (1994). *Forest landscape design guidelines.* HMSO, London.

FORESTRY AUTHORITY (1998). *The UK Forestry Standard: The government's approach to sustainable forestry.* Forestry Commission, Edinburgh.

FORESTRY COMMISSION (1991). *Community woodland design guidelines.* HMSO, London.

FORESTRY COMMISSION (1999). *Managing deer in the countryside.* Practice Note 6. Forestry Commission, Edinburgh.

FORESTRY COMMISSION (2000). *Forests & water guidelines*, 3rd edn. Forestry Commission, Edinburgh.

FORESTRY COMMISSION (in prep.). *Forest roads.* Forestry Practice Guide. Forestry Commission, Edinburgh.

FRAZER, D. (1983). *Amphibians and reptiles in Britain.* Collins, London.

FULLER, R.J. (1991). Effects of woodland edges on songbirds. In: *Edge management in woodlands*, ed. R. Ferris-Kaan. Forestry Commission Occasional Paper 28. Forestry Commission, Edinburgh, 31–34.

FULLER, R.J. and LANGSLOW, D.R. (1984). Estimating the numbers of birds by point counts: how long should the counts last? *Bird Study* **31**, 195–202.

FULLER, R.J. and WARREN, M.S. (1993). *Coppiced woodlands: their management for wildlife.* Joint Nature Conservation Committee, Peterborough.

FULLER, R.J. and WHITTINGTON, P.A. (1987). Breeding bird distribution within Lincolnshire ash–lime woodlands: the influence of rides and the woodland edge. *Acta Oecologica/Oecologica Generalis* **8**, 259–268.

GARDINER, B.A. and STACEY, G.R. (1996). *Designing forest edges to improve wind stability.* Technical Paper 16. Forestry Commission, Edinburgh.

GATES, J.E. and GYSEL, L.W. (1978). Avian nest dispersion and fledging success in field–forest ecotones. *Ecology* **59**(5), 871–883.

GILL, R.M.A. (1991a). Grazing animals: their impact and potential value in ride management. In: *Edge management in woodlands*, ed. R. Ferris-Kaan. Forestry Commission Occasional Paper 28. Forestry Commission, Edinburgh, 49–56.

GILL, R.M.A. (1991b). A review of damage by mammals in northern temperate forests. 1: Deer. *Forestry* **65**(2), 154–171.

GREATOREX-DAVIES, J.N. (1991). Woodland edge management for invertebrates. In: *Edge management in woodlands*, ed. R. Ferris-Kaan. Forestry Commission Occasional Paper 28. Forestry Commission, Edinburgh, 25–30.

GREATOREX-DAVIES, J.N., HALL, M.L. and MARRS, R.H. (1992). The conservation of the pearl-bordered fritillary butterfly (*Boloria euphrosyne* L.): preliminary studies on the creation and management of glades in conifer plantations. *Forest Ecology and Management* **53**, 1–14.

GREATOREX-DAVIES, J.N., SPARKS, T.H. and HALL, M.L. (1994). The response of *Heteroptera* and *Coleoptera* species to shade and aspect in rides of coniferised lowland woods in southern England. *Biological Conservation* **67**, 255–273.

GREEN, L.R. and NEWELL, L.A. (1982). Using goats to control brush regrowth on fuelbreaks. USDA Forest Service, Pacific Southwest Forest and Range Experiment Station. General Technical Report PSW-59.

GRIME, J.P. (1979). *Plant strategies and vegetation processes*. John Wiley, Chichester.

GRIME, J.P., HODGSON, J.G. and HUNT, R. (1988). *Comparative plant ecology*. Unwin Hyman, London.

GURNELL, J. (1985). Woodland rodent communities. In: *The ecology of woodland rodents, bank voles and wood mice*, ed. J.R. Flowerdew, J. Gurnell and J.H.W. Gipps. Symposia of the Zoological Society of London No. 55. Oxford University Press, Oxford, 377–411.

GURNELL, J. and FLOWERDEW, J.R. (1994). *Live trapping small mammals: a practical guide*. Occasional Publication of The Mammal Society No.3. The Mammal Society, London.

HALL, M.L. and GREATOREX-DAVIES, J.N. (1989). Management guidelines for the conservation of invertebrates, especially butterflies, in plantation woodland. Unpublished Nature Conservancy Council, Natural Environment Research Council Contract Report (HF3/08/12).

HANSEN, J.A. (1986). Experience in the use of livestock to control gorse in Ashley Forest. *Proceedings Agroforestry Symposium*, 24-27 November 1986. *FRI Bulletin* **139**, 85–94.

HANSSON, L. (1977). Landscape ecology and stability of populations. *Landscape Planning* **4**, 85–93.

HANSSON, L. (1983). Bird numbers across edges between mature conifer forest and clearcuts in Central Sweden. *Ornis Scandinavica* **14**, 97–103.

HARRIS, L.D. (1984). *The fragmented forest: island biogeography theory and the preservation of biotic diversity*. University of Chicago Press, Chicago and London.

HEATH, J. (1965). A genuinely portable u.v. light trap. *Entomologist's Record* **77**, 236–238.

HILL, M.O. (1979). The development of a flora in even-aged plantation. In: *The ecology of even-aged forest plantations*, ed. E.D. Ford, D.C. Malcolm and J Atterson. IUFRO, Edinburgh, 175–192.

HUMPHREY, J.W., GILL, R.M.A. and CLARIDGE, J., eds (1998). *Grazing as a management tool in European forest ecosystems*. Technical Paper 25. Forestry Commission, Edinburgh.

HUNTER, M.L. (1990). *Wildlife, forests, and forestry: principles of managing forests for biological diversity*. Prentice Hall, New Jersey.

KIRBY, K.J. (1995). *Rebuilding the English countryside: habitat fragmentation and wildlife corridors as issues in practical conservation*. English Nature Science No. 10. English Nature, Peterborough.

LEE, R. (1978). *Forest microclimatology*. Columbia University Press, New York.

LEOPOLD, A. (1933). *Game management*. Scribner, New York.

LEWIS, T. and TAYLOR, L.R. (1967). *Introduction to experimental ecology*. Academic Press, London.

LUKEN, J.O. (1990). *Directing ecological succession*. Chapman and Hall, London.

LUKEN, J.O., HINTON, A.C. and BAKER, D.G. (1991). Forest edges associated with power-line corridors and implications for corridor siting. *Landscape and Urban Planning* **20**, 315–324.

MCCARTHY, R.B. (1985). Use of goats to control blackberries and undergrowth within *P. radiata* and *E. regnans* plantations of APM forests, Gippsland, Victoria. ANZIF Conference, May 1985, Hobart, Tasmania, 197–204.

MCKINNELL, F.H. (1975). Control of weeds in radiata pine plantations by sheep grazing. *Australian Forest Research* **6**(4), 1–4.

MARSHALL, E.J.P. (1983). *A feasibility study of the use of chemicals for rural amenity areas*. Technical Report, Agricultural Research Council, Weed Research Organisation, Oxford, 71.

MATLACK, G.R. (1993). Microenvironment variation within and among forest edge sites in the eastern United States. *Biological Conservation* **66**, 185–194.

MAYLE, B.A. (1990). *Habitat management for woodland bats.* Research Information Note 165. Forestry Commission, Farnham.

MAYLE, B.A. (1996). Progress in predictive management of deer populations in British woodlands. *Forest Ecology and Management* **88**, 187–198.

MAYLE, B.A. (1999). *Domestic stock grazing to enhance woodland biodiversity.* Information Note 28. Forestry Commission, Edinburgh.

MAYLE, B.A. and GURNELL, J. (1991). Edge management and small mammals. In: *Edge management in woodlands*, ed. R. Ferris-Kaan. Forestry Commission Occasional Paper 28. Forestry Commission, Edinburgh, 42-48.

MILES, J. (1979). *Vegetation dynamics.* Outline Studies in Ecology. Chapman and Hall, London.

MITCHELL, B., STAINES, B.W. and WELCH, D. (1977). *Ecology of red deer: a research review relevant to their management in Scotland.* ITE, Cambridge.

MITCHELL, P.L. (1992). Growth stages and microclimate in coppice and high forest. In: *Ecology and management of coppice woodlands*, ed. G.P. Buckley. Chapman and Hall, London, 31–51.

MITCHELL, P.L. and KIRBY, K.J. (1989). *Ecological effects of forestry practices in long-established woodland and their implications for nature conservation.* Oxford Forestry Institute Occasional Paper No. 39. Nature Conservancy Council/University of Oxford, Oxford.

MONTGOMERY, W.I. (1987). *The application of capture-mark-recapture methods to the enumeration of small mammal populations.* Symposia of the Zoological Society of London No. 58. Oxford University Press, London, 25–57.

MORRIS, P.A. (1991). Family Gliridae (dormice) – common dormouse, *Muscardinus avellanarius*. In: *The handbook of British mammals*, ed. G. B. Corbet and S. Harris. Blackwell Scientific, Oxford, 259–264.

MÜLLER, H. (1883). *The fertilisation of flowers.* Translation by D'Arcy W. Thompson. London.

ODUM, E.P. (1971). *Fundamentals of ecology*, 3rd edn. Saunders, Philadelphia.

O'TOOLE, C. and RAW, A. (1991). *Bees of the world.* Blandford, London.

PARR, T.W. (1988). Long-term effects of grass growth retardants, with particular reference to the ecology and management of vegetation on roadside verges. *Aspects of Applied Biology* **16**, 35–45.

PATMORE, J.M. (1990). Ride cutting in ancient woodland plantations: benefits for nature conservation. MSc Thesis, Wye College, University of London.

PETERKEN, G.F. (1991). Managing semi-natural woods: a suitable case for coppice. *Quarterly Journal of Forestry* **84**, 21–29.

PETERKEN, G.F. (1993). *Woodland conservation and management*, 2nd edn. Chapman and Hall, London.

PETTY, S.J. and AVERY. M.I. (1990). *Forest bird communities.* Occasional Paper 26. Forestry Commission, Edinburgh.

PIETZARKA, U. and ROLOFF, A. (1993). Waldrandgestaltung unter Berücksichtigung der natürlichen Vegetationsdynamik. *Forstarchiv* **64**, 107–113.

POLLARD, E. (1977). A method for assessing changes in the abundance of butterflies. *Biological Conservation* **12**, 115–134.

POLLARD, E. (1979). Population ecology and change in range of the white admiral butterfly *Ladoga camilla* L. in England. *Ecological Entomology* **4**, 61–74.

POLLARD, E., HALL, M.L. and BIBBY, T.J. (1986). *Monitoring the abundance of butterflies, 1976-1985.* Nature Conservancy Council, Peterborough.

POLLARD, E. and YATES, T. (1993). *Monitoring butterflies for ecology and conservation.* Chapman and Hall, London.

PORTER, K. (1993). Wide rides for butterflies. *Enact* **1**(1), 17–19.

PUTMAN, R.J. (1996). Ungulates in temperate forest ecosystems: perspectives and recommendations for future research. *Forest Ecology and Management* **88**, 205–214.

QUINE, C.P. and GARDINER, B.A. (1992). *Incorporating the threat of windthrow into forest design plans*. Forestry Commission Research Information Note 220. Forestry Authority, Farnham.

RACKHAM, O. (1975). Temperatures of plant communities as measured by pyrometric and other methods. In: *Light as an ecological factor: II*, ed. G.C. Evans, R. Bainbridge and O. Rackham. Blackwell Scientific Publications, Oxford, 423–449.

RANNEY, J.W., BRUNER, M.C. and LEVENSON, J.B. (1981). The importance of edge in the structure and dynamics of forest islands. In: *Forest island dynamics in man-dominated landscapes*, ed. R.L. Burgess and D.M. Sharpe. Ecological Studies 41. Springer-Verlag, New York, 67-95.

RATCLIFFE, P.R. (1985). *Glades for deer control in upland forests*. Forestry Commission Leaflet 86. HMSO, London.

RATCLIFFE, P.R. (1987). *The management of red deer in upland forests*. Forestry Commission Bulletin 71. HMSO, London.

ROBERTSON, P.A. (1992). *Woodland management for pheasants*. Forestry Commission Bulletin 106. HMSO, London.

ROBINSON, H.S. (1952). On the behaviour of night-flying insects in the neighbourhood of a bright source of light. *Proceedings of the Royal Entomological Society of London* **27**, 13–21.

ROWAN, A.A. (1976). *Forest road planning*. Forestry Commission Booklet 43. HMSO, London.

SHARROW, S.H., LEININGER, W.C. and RHODES, B. (1989). Sheep grazing as a silvicultural tool to suppress brush. *Journal of Range Management* **42**(1), 2–4.

SNOW, B. and SNOW, D. (1988). *Birds and berries*. Poyser, Calton, Staffordshire.

SOUTHERN, H.N., ed. (1964). *The handbook of British mammals*. Blackwell Scientific Publications, Oxford.

SOUTHWOOD, T.R.E. (1978). *Ecological methods with particular reference to the study of insect populations*. Chapman and Hall, London.

SPARKS, T.H. and GREATOREX-DAVIES, J.N. (1992). The effect of shade in plantation woodland on invertebrate abundance and diversity. *Aspects of Applied Biology* **29**, 89–96.

SPARKS, T.H., GREATOREX-DAVIES, J.N., MOUNTFORD, J.O., HALL, M.L. and MARRS, R.H. (1996). The effects of shade on the plant communities of rides in plantation woodland and implications for butterfly conservation. *Forest Ecology and Management* **80**, 197–207.

SPELLERBERG, I.F. and GAYWOOD, M.J. (1993). *Linear features: linear habitats and wildlife corridors*. English Nature Research Report No.60. English Nature, Peterborough.

SPENCER, J.W. and KIRBY, K.J. (1992). An inventory of ancient woodland for England and Wales. *Biological Conservation* **62**, 77–93.

STEEL, C. and KHAN, R. (1986). The management of rides and open spaces. Internal Forestry Commission Report. Forestry Commission, West England.

THOMAS, J.A. (1984). The conservation of butterflies in temperate countries : past efforts and lessons for the future. In: *The biology of butterflies*, ed. R.I. Vane-Wright and P.A. Ackery. Academic Press, London, 334–353.

THOMAS, J.A. (1989). *Butterflies of the British Isles*. Hamlyn, London.

THOMAS, R.E. and KIRBY, K.J. (1992). 17 years of change in the structure and composition of Wytham Woods (Oxfordshire). *Aspects of Applied Biology* **29**, 49–55.

THORNBER, K.A. (1993). An assessment of the impact of some vertebrate herbivores on regeneration in newly-created lowland forest rides. Unpublished Research Report. Forestry Authority (Research Division), Farnham.

UK GOVERNMENT (1994a). *Biodiversity: the UK action plan*. HMSO, London.

UK GOVERNMENT (1994b). *Sustainable forestry: the UK programme*. HMSO, London.

ULERY, A.L., GRAHAM, R.C. and AMRHEIN, C. (1993). Wood-ash composition and soil pH following intense burning. *Soil Science* **156**, 358–364.

VALENTINE, D.H. (1949). Vegetative and cytological variation in *Viola riviniana*. In: *British flowering plants and modern systematic methods*, ed. A.J. Wilmott. BSBI Conference Report No.1. Botanical Society of the British Isles, London, 48.

VERKAAR, H.J. (1990). Corridors as a tool for plant species conservation? In: *Species dispersal in agricultural habitats*, ed. R.G.H. Bunce and D.C. Howard. Belhaven Press, London, 82–97.

WARREN, M.S. (1985). The influence of shade on butterfly numbers in woodland rides, with special reference to the wood white, *Leptidea sinapis*. *Biological Conservation* **33**, 147–1645.

WARREN, M.S. (1987a). The ecology and conservation of the heath fritillary butterfly, *Mellicta athalia*. I. Host selection and phenology. *Journal of Applied Ecology* **24**, 467–482.

WARREN, M.S. (1987b). The ecology and conservation of the heath fritillary butterfly, *Mellicta athalia*. II. Adult population structure and mobility. *Journal of Applied Ecology* **24**, 483–498.

WARREN, M.S. and FULLER, R.J. (1993). *Woodland rides and glades: their management for wildlife*. Joint Nature Conservation Committee, Peterborough.

WATT, T.A., KIRBY, K.J. and SAVILL, P.S. (1988). Effects of herbicides on woodland plant communities. *Aspects of Applied Biology* **16**, 383–392.

WHITTAKER, R.H. (1972). Evolution and the measurement of species diversity. *Taxon* **21**, 213–251.

WILLIAMS, C.B. (1948). The Rothamsted light trap. *Proceedings of the Royal Entomological Society of London* **23**, 80–85.

WILLIAMS-LINERA, G. (1990). Vegetation structure and environmental conditions of forest edges in Panama. *Journal of Ecology* **78**, 356–373.

WILLIS, A.J. (1991). On the verges of discovery at Bibury. *NERC News*, April 1991, 28–30.

WILLOUGHBY, I. and DEWAR, J. (1995). *The use of herbicides in the forest*. Forestry Commission Field Book 8. HMSO, London.

WOLTON, R.J. and FLOWERDEW, J.R. (1985). Spatial distribution and movements of wood mice, yellow-necked mice and bank voles. In: *The ecology of woodland rodents, bank voles and wood mice*, ed. J.R. Flowerdew, J. Gurnell and J.H.W. Gipps. Symposia of the Zoological Society of London No. 55. Oxford University Press, Oxford, 249–275.

WOODBURN, M.I.A. (1991). Gamebirds and woodland edges. In: *Edge management in woodlands*, ed. R. Ferris-Kaan. Forestry Commission Occasional Paper 28. Forestry Commission, Edinburgh, 35–41.

YAHNER, R.H. (1988). Changes in wildlife communities near edges. *Conservation Biology* **2**, 333–339.

YALLOP, B.D. and HOHENKERK, C.Y. (1991). Modelling light conditions in woodland rides. In: *Edge management in woodlands*, ed. R. Ferris-Kaan. Forestry Commission Occasional Paper 28. Forestry Commission, Edinburgh, 11–16.

YOUNG, J.B. and GORDON, I.J. (1991). The potential for domestic stock grazing for wildlife conservation in forests. Unpublished MLURI report for Forestry Commission.

Appendix 1

Scientific names for animal species mentioned in the text

Adder	*Vipera berus*
Adonis blue	*Lysandra bellargus*
Ants	*Lasius* spp.
Bank vole	*Clethrionomys glareolus*
Blackbird	*Turdus merula*
Blackcap	*Sylvia atricapilla*
Black hairstreak	*Strymonidia pruni*
Brown argus	*Aricia agestis*
Brown hairstreak	*Thecla betulae*
Chaffinch	*Fringilla coelebs*
Chalkhill blue	*Lysandra coridon*
Chequered skipper	*Carterocephalus palaemon*
Chiff-chaff	*Phylloscopus collybita*
Clouded yellow	*Colias croceus*
Comma	*Polygonia c-album*
Common blue	*Polyommatus icarus*
Common dormouse	*Muscardinus avellanarius*
Common frog	*Rana temporaria*
Common lizard	*Lacerta vivipara*
Cuckoo	*Cuculus canorus*
Dark green fritillary	*Argynnis aglaja*
Dingy skipper	*Erynnis tages*
Duke of Burgundy fritillary	*Hamearis lucina*
Essex skipper	*Thymelicus lineola*
Fallow deer	*Dama dama*
Field vole	*Microtus agrestis*
Fox	*Vulpes vulpes*
Garden warbler	*Sylvia borin*
Gatekeeper	*Pyronia tithonus*
Glanville fritillary	*Melitaea cinxia*
Grass snake	*Natrix natrix*
Grayling	*Hipparchia semele*
Green hairstreak	*Callophrys rubi*
Green-veined white	*Pieris napi*

Green woodpecker	*Picus viridis*
Grizzled skipper	*Pyrgus malvae*
Hare	*Lepus europaeus*
High brown fritillary	*Argynnis adippe*
Heath fritillary	*Mellicta athalia*
Holly blue	*Celastrina argiolus*
Kestrel	*Falco tinnunculus*
Large blue	*Maculinea arion*
Large copper	*Lycaena dispar*
Large heath	*Coenonympha tullia*
Large skipper	*Ochlodes venata*
Large tortoiseshell	*Nymphalis polychloros*
Large white	*Pieris brassicae*
Large wood ants	*Formica* spp.
Lulworth skipper	*Thymelicus acteon*
Marbled white	*Melanargia galathea*
Marsh fritillary	*Eurodryas aurinia*
Meadow brown	*Maniola jurtina*
Mountain ringlet	*Erebia epiphron*
Muntjac	*Muntiacus reevesi*
Nightingale	*Luscinia megarhynchos*
Northern brown argus	*Aricia artaxerxes*
Orange tip	*Anthocharis cardamines*
Painted lady	*Cynthia cardui*
Peacock	*Inachis io*
Pearl-bordered fritillary	*Boloria euphrosyne*
Pheasant	*Phasianus colchicus*
Purple emperor	*Apatura iris*
Purple hairstreak	*Quercusia quercus*
Rabbit	*Oryctolagus cuninculus*
Red admiral	*Vanessa atalanta*
Red deer	*Cervus elaphus*
Ringlet	*Aphantopus hyperantus*
Robin	*Erithacus rubecula*
Roe deer	*Capreolus capreolus*
Sand lizard	*Lacerta agilis*
Scotch argus	*Erebia aethiops*
Shrews	*Sorex* spp.
Sika deer	*Cervus nippon*

Silver-spotted skipper	*Hesperia comma*
Silver-studded blue	*Plebejus argus*
Silver-washed fritillary	*Argynnis paphia*
Small blue	*Cupido minimus*
Small copper	*Lycaena phlaeas*
Small heath	*Coenonympha pamphilus*
Small pearl-bordered fritillary	*Boloria selene*
Small skipper	*Thymelicus sylvestris*
Small tortoiseshell	*Aglais urticae*
Small white	*Pieris rapae*
Song thrush	*Turdus philomelos*
Sparrowhawk	*Accipiter nisus*
Speckled wood	*Pararge aegeria*
Stoat	*Mustela nivalis*
Swallowtail	*Papilio machaon*
Tawny owl	*Strix aluco*
Thrushes	*Turdus* spp.
Tits	*Parus* spp.
Wall brown	*Lasiommata megera*
Weasel	*Mustela nivalis*
White admiral	*Ladoga camilla*
White-letter hairstreak	*Strymonidia w-album*
Willow warbler	*Phylloscopus trochilus*
Wood mice	*Apodemus sylvaticus*
Wood white	*Leptidea sinapis*

Appendix 2

Scientific names for plant species mentioned in the text

Alder	*Alnus glutinosa*
Ash	*Fraxinus excelsior*
Barren brome	*Bromus sterilis*
Beech	*Fagus sylvaticus*
Bellflowers	*Campanula* spp.
Bell heather	*Erica cinerea*
Betony	*Betonica officinalis*
Bilberry/Blaeberry	*Vaccinium myrtillus*
Birch	*Betula* spp.
Bird cherry	*Prunus padus*
Bird's-foot trefoil	*Lotus corniculatus*
Bitter vetch	*Lathyrus montanus*
Black bent-grass	*Agrostis gigantea*
Black knapweed	*Centaurea nigra*
Black medick	*Medicago lupulina*
Black spleenwort	*Asplenium adiantum-nigrum*
Blackthorn	*Prunus spinosa*
Bluebell	*Hyacinthoides non-scripta*
Bracken	*Pteridium aquilinum*
Bramble	*Rubus fruticosus* agg.
Broad buckler-fern	*Dryopteris dilatata*
Broadleaved dock	*Rumex obtusifolius*
Broadleaved helleborine	*Epipactis helleborine*
Broadleaved willowherb	*Epilobium montanum*
Broom	*Sarothamnus scoparius*
Brown knapweed	*Centaurea jacea*
Buckthorn	*Rhamnus catharticus*
Bugle	*Ajuga reptans*
Burnet saxifrage	*Pimpinella saxifraga*
Buttercups	*Ranunculus* spp.
Caraway	*Carum carvi*
Cleavers	*Galium aparine*
Clustered dock	*Rumex conglomeratus*
Cocksfoot	*Dactylis glomerata*

Common bent-grass	*Agrostis capillaris*
Common cow-wheat	*Melampyrum pratense*
Common dog-violet	*Viola riviniana*
Common nettle (syn. stinging nettle)	*Urtica dioica*
Common ragwort	*Senecio jacobaea*
Common rush	*Juncus conglomeratus*
Common sedge	*Carex nigra*
Common Solomon's seal	*Polygonatum multiflorum*
Common stork's-bill	*Erodium cicutarium*
Common twayblade	*Listera ovata*
Corsican pine	*Pinus nigra* var. *maritima*
Cow parsley	*Anthriscus sylvestris*
Cowslip	*Primula veris*
Cranberry	*Vaccinium oxycoccus*
Creeping bent	*Agrostis stolonifera*
Creeping buttercup	*Ranunculus repens*
Creeping cinquefoil	*Potentilla reptans*
Creeping soft-grass	*Holcus mollis*
Creeping thistle	*Cirsium arvense*
Creeping willow	*Salix repens*
Cross-leaved heath	*Erica tetralix*
Cuckooflower (syn. lady's smock)	*Cardamine pratensis*
Currants	*Ribes* spp.
Dandelion	*Taraxacum* agg.
Devil's bit-scabious	*Succisa pratensis*
Dill	*Anethum graveolens*
Dog's mercury	*Mercurialis perennis*
Dogwood	*Thelycrania sanguinea*
Douglas fir	*Pseudotsuga menziesii*
Downy birch	*Betula pubescens*
Dwarf gorse	*Ulex minor*
Enchanter's nightshade	*Circaea lutetiana*
False oat-grass	*Arrhenatherum elatius*
False brome	*Brachypodium sylvaticum*
Fescues	*Festuca* spp.
Field scabious	*Knautia arvensis*
Field maple	*Acer campestre*
Fleabane	*Pulicaria dysenterica*
Foxglove	*Digitalis purpurea*

Garlic mustard	*Alliaria petiolata*
Germander speedwell	*Veronica chamaedrys*
Gorse	*Ulex* spp.
Grass-of-Parnassus	*Parnassia palustris*
Great mullein	*Verbascum thapsus*
Great wood-rush	*Luzula sylvatica*
Greater bird's-foot trefoil	*Lotus pedunculatus*
Greater stitchwort	*Stellaria holostea*
Grey willow	*Salix cinerea* agg.
Ground elder	*Aegopodium podograria*
Ground ivy	*Glechoma hederacea*
Guelder rose	*Viburnum opulus*
Hard-fern	*Blechnum spicant*
Hare's-tail cottongrass	*Eriophorum vaginatum*
Hairy St John's wort	*Hypericum hirsutum*
Hairy wood-rush	*Luzula pilosa*
Hawkweed ox-tongue	*Picris hieracioides*
Hawthorn	*Crataegus monogyna*
Hazel	*Corylus avellana*
Heath bedstraw	*Galium saxatile*
Heath rush	*Juncus squarrosus*
Heather	*Calluna vulgaris*
Heath groundsel	*Senecio sylvaticus*
Hedge bedstraw	*Galium mollugo*
Hedge woundwort	*Stachys sylvatica*
Hemp agrimony	*Eupatorium cannibinum*
Herb Bennet	*Geum urbanum*
Herb Robert	*Geranium robertianum*
Hogweed	*Heracleum sphondylium*
Holly	*Ilex aquifolium*
Honeysuckle	*Lonicera periclymenum*
Hornbeam	*Carpinus betulus*
Hybrid cinquefoil	*Potentilla* x *mixta*
Hybrid larch	*Larix* x *eurolepis*
Ivy	*Hedera helix*
Knapweeds	*Centaurea* spp.
Knotgrass	*Polygonum aviculare*
Lady-fern	*Athyrium filix-femina*
Lady's smock (syn. cuckooflower)	*Cardamine pratensis*

Larch	*Larix* spp.
Lesser burdock	*Arctium minus*
Lesser celandine	*Ranunculus ficaria*
Lesser twayblade	*Listera chordata*
Lime	*Tilia* spp.
Lodgepole pine	*Pinus contorta*
Lungwort	*Pulmonaria officinalis*
Marsh thistle	*Cirsium palustre*
Mat grass	*Nardus stricta*
Meadow vetchling	*Lathyrus pratensis*
Moschatel	*Adoxa moschatellina*
Narrow buckler-fern	*Dryopteris carthusiana*
Norway maple	*Acer platanoides*
Norway spruce	*Picea abies*
Ox-eye daisy	*Chrysanthemum leucanthemum*
Pale willowherb	*Epilobium roseum*
Pedunculate oak	*Quercus robur*
Perforate St John's wort	*Hypericum perforatum*
Pignut	*Conopodium majus*
Pill-headed sedge	*Carex pilulifera*
Primrose	*Primula vulgaris*
Purple moor-grass	*Molinia caerulea*
Purple small-reed	*Calamagrostis epigeos*
Ragged robin	*Lychnis flos-cuculi*
Ragwort	*Senecio* spp.
Red fescue	*Festuca rubra*
Ribwort plantain	*Plantago lanceolata*
Rosebay willowherb	*Epilobium angustifolium*
Rough chervil	*Chaerophyllum temulentum*
Rough hawkbit	*Leontodon hispidus*
Rough meadow-grass	*Poa trivialis*
Rowan	*Sorbus aucuparia*
Sallow	*Salix caprea*
Scaly male-fern	*Dryopteris affinis*
Scots pine	*Pinus sylvestris*
Sheep's fescue	*Festuca ovina*
Silver birch	*Betula pendula*
Silver fir	*Abies alba*
Sitka spruce	*Picea sitchensis*

Slender St John's wort	*Hypericum pulchrum*
Smooth-stalked sedge	*Carex laevigata*
Soft rush	*Juncus effusus*
Spear-leaved willowherb	*Epilobium lanceolatum*
Speedwell	*Veronica* spp.
Spindle	*Euonymus europaeus*
Square-stalked willowherb	*Epilobium tetragonum*
Stinging nettle (syn. common nettle)	*Urtica dioica*
Sweet vernal-grass	*Anthoxanthum odoratum*
Sycamore	*Acer pseudoplatanus*
Tall fescue	*Festuca arundinacea*
Tansy	*Chrysanthemum vulgare*
Thistles	*Cirsium* or *Carduus* spp.
Three-veined sandwort	*Moehringia trinervia*
Timothy	*Phleum pratense*
Tormentil	*Potentilla erecta*
Trailing St John's wort	*Hypericum humifusum*
Traveller's joy/old man's beard	*Clematis vitalba*
Tufted hair-grass	*Deschampsia cespitosa*
Tufted vetch	*Vicia cracca*
Valerian	*Valeriana officinalis*
Velvet bent-grass	*Agrostis canina*
Violet helliborine	*Epipactis purpurata*
Violets	*Viola* spp.
Water parsnip	*Sium latifolium*
Wavy hair-grass	*Deschampsia flexuosa*
Wayfaring tree	*Viburnum lantana*
Weld	*Reseda luteola*
Welted thistle	*Carduus acanthoides*
White bryony	*Bryonia dioica*
White dead-nettle	*Lamium album*
Wild angelica	*Angelica sylvestris*
Wild carrot	*Daucus carota*
Wild cherry	*Prunus avium*
Wild mignonette	*Reseda lutea*
Wild privet	*Ligustrum vulgare*
Wild strawberry	*Fragaria vesca*
Willowherbs	*Epilobium* spp.
Willows	*Salix* spp.

Wood anemone	*Anemone nemorosa*
Wood dock	*Rumex sanguineus*
Wood meadow-grass	*Poa nemoralis*
Wood melick	*Melica uniflora*
Wood millet	*Milium effusum*
Wood sedge	*Carex sylvatica*
Wood sorrel	*Oxalis acetosella*
Wood speedwell	*Veronica montana*
Wood spurge	*Euphorbia amygdaloides*
Yarrow	*Achillea millefolium*
Yellow archangel	*Lamiastrum galeobdolon*
Yellow loosestrife	*Lysimachia vulgaris*
Yellow pimpernel	*Lysimachia nemorum*
Yorkshire fog	*Holcus lanatus*

Printed by Colourgraphic Arts, Bordon, Hampshire.